When It's Over

When It's Over

Allie Iglesias

Bald and Bonkers Network LLC

Contents

First Printing, 2023

ISBN/SKU:979-8-8689-2392-0

EISBN: 979-8-8689-2393-7

Introduction

Have you ever found yourself wondering why some relationships - whether they be romantic, platonic, or even professional - tend to lose their spark over time, leaving us feeling disconnected and disheartened? Why is it that once seamless connections now seem like obstacles, leaving us longing for something more? Life has a way of presenting us with these challenges, forcing us to navigate the delicate art of letting go. But fear not, dear reader, for within the pages of this book, I will guide you through the labyrinth of emotions, revelations, and personal growth that come with the end of a relationship, no matter how significant or insignificant it may seem.

"When It's Over" is an engrossing journey through the complexities of recognizing when a relationship has run its course and gracefully stepping away. Throughout this book, I will delve deeply into the realms of friendships, family ties, romance, and even the intricacies of the workplace, shedding light on the signs that indicate when it's time to bid farewell.

But let me be clear - this is not a tale of despair or heartbreak. Instead, it is a beacon of hope, a compassionate guide for those feeling stuck in the stagnant waters of a relationship that no longer serves them. It is an exploration of self-discovery and a testament to the resilience of our human nature.

In the enchanting world of our daily lives, we often find ourselves entangled in the webs of routine, routines that can gradually blind us to the truth. We become so accustomed to the familiar faces and comfortable spaces that we forget to question whether they truly bring us joy. It's as if we've been living in a realm of colorless hues, an existence that dampens our spirit.

But fear not, for I will paint the canvas of your life with vibrant shades of possibility. Together, we will navigate the intricacies of identifying when a relationship has lost its spark and discover the courage to let go gracefully.

In the realm of friendships, I will guide you through the bittersweet realization that not all bonds are meant to last forever. As we grow and evolve, our values and interests may diverge, leading us down different paths. But in bidding farewell to a fading friendship, we create space for new connections to blossom, ones that align with our authentic selves.

Within the realm of family ties, I will accompany you through the challenging process of redefining boundaries and finding harmony amidst the complexity of familial love. Sometimes, it is necessary to acknowledge that certain dynamics no longer serve our wellbeing, and in doing so, we carve a path towards healing and growth.

In matters of romance, I will gently unravel the layers of disappointment and disillusionment that often accompany the end of a love story. We will explore the importance of self-reflection, recognizing patterns, and ultimately embracing the freedom that comes with walking away from a relationship that no longer nourishes our souls.

Within the intricate web of the workplace, I will provide insights and strategies for navigating the sometimes treacherous waters of professional relationships. Together, we will uncover the signs that indicate a toxic work environment, allowing you to step into your power and seek opportunities that ignite your passion.

Through heartfelt anecdotes, practical exercises, and soul-stirring reflections, "When It's Over" will be your steadfast companion during this transformative journey. It will empower you to release attachments that hinder your growth and courageously embrace the limitless possibilities that await.

Remember, dear reader, the end of a relationship does not signify failure but rather an invitation to rediscover your own worth and resilience. It is an opportunity to embark on a profound voyage of self-love, acceptance, and new beginnings.

So gather your strength, sharpen your intuition, and join me as we embark on an adventure of self-discovery. Together, we will dare to let go of what no longer serves us and create a life that is vibrant, meaningful, and true to our hearts. Let "When It's Over" be your guiding light in the darkness, illuminating the path towards a future filled with self-empowerment, growth, and a love that knows no bounds.

But fear not, dear reader, for awakening awaits. Like a dormant flower bathed in the morning light, we too have the power to blossom and flourish, even after enduring the darkest storms. "When It's Over" is here to remind you of the infinite possibilities that lie beyond the boundaries of a relationship that has reached its end.

Imagine this: you find yourself standing at the edge of a vast emerald meadow, the sun casting a warm glow upon your weary face. With each breath, the intoxicating scent of wildflowers stirs in the air, gently urging you to embark on this transformative journey. As you step into the unknown, shedding the weight of what no longer serves you, you are embraced by a sense of liberation and a profound exploration of self-discovery.

The meadow becomes more than just a physical space; it transforms into a portal of endless opportunities and limitless potential. As you wander deeper into its depths, the melody of nature surrounds you, soothing your soul and guiding your steps.

In this expansive sanctuary, the past becomes a distant memory, fading into the background like a fleeting dream. You embark on a quest for self-love, self-renewal, and self-redefinition. It is a time of reflection and introspection, where you uncover the layers of who you truly are, untethered from the constraints of a fading relationship.

You encounter a hidden waterfall, its cascading torrents symbolizing the release of emotions that may have been suppressed for far too long. As the cool water rejuvenates and revitalizes your spirit, you find solace in the acceptance of your emotions, understanding that healing comes from allowing yourself to feel, to grieve, and to grow.

The journey takes you through enchanted forests, where wise trees whisper ancient wisdom and lend a listening ear to the secrets you need to share. They remind you that you possess an inner strength, a resilience that will guide you through the challenging moments still to come.

As you travel onwards, you stumble upon a field of mirrors, each reflecting back moments of joy, laughter, and love. Within them, you witness the person you were and the person you are becoming. Reminded of your worth and the qualities that make you unique, you embrace the power of self-acceptance and forgiveness.

With every step, you leave traces of your old self behind, shedding the skin of past insecurities and doubts. You emerge from the meadow, not as a broken soul, but as a vibrant and radiant being, ready to seize the world with renewed vigor.

For you have discovered that the end of a relationship is not an end at all, but a new beginning. It is a chance to reinvent yourself, to chase dreams that were once put on hold, and to weave the tapestry of your own destiny.

So, dear reader, let go of the remnants of a love that has run its course. Embrace the transformative power that lies within you. Set sail on the vast sea of possibilities, for as you step into the light of your awakening, you realize that the best chapters of your life are yet to be written.

Together, we will navigate the labyrinth of emotions that often accompany the conclusion of a relationship. We will unravel the threads that tie us to toxicity and weave a tapestry of resilience and growth. Through introspection, guided exercises, and heartwarming anecdotes, we will untangle the intricate knots of confusion, fear, and doubt that cloud our judgment.

Picture the cathartic release that comes with letting go. Feel the lightness that envelopes you as you shed the layers of expectations, obligations, and heartache. "When It's Over" is your passport to this transformative experience, a blueprint for reclaiming your authentic self and embracing the untapped potential that lies within.

By the time you turn the final page of this thought-provoking journey, you will emerge as a beacon of strength, armed with the wisdom and compassion needed to not only recognize when it's time to step away but to do so with grace and integrity. Whether you find yourself entangled in a toxic friendship, a suffocating romantic bond, or a business partnership that no longer aligns with your values, "When It's Over" will be your companion, your guiding star, leading you towards the light of a brighter future.

So, my dear reader, are you ready to embark on this transformative expedition through the depths of human connection and personal growth? Are you ready to embrace the compassion of letting go and prepare for your own rebirth? If your heart whispers "yes," then set aside any doubts and open these pages with a sense of anticipation. An adventure awaits.

But fear not, for this book will awaken your senses and open your eyes to the vibrant spectrum of possibilities that await you. Through introspection, reflection, and gentle guidance, I will help you peel back the layers of complacency and rediscover the essence of who you are and what you truly deserve.

Together, we will embark on a journey of exploration, uncovering the reasons behind the waning spark in your relationships. We will delve into the intricacies of communication, the role of personal growth, and the power dynamics that often shape our connections. Through stories of triumph and revelation, we will witness others who have traversed the path of letting go and emerged stronger on the other side.

In these pages, you will find practical advice, actionable steps, and thought-provoking exercises that will empower you to make decisions that align with your highest good. You will learn to listen to the whispers of your heart and trust the guidance it provides. You will understand that parting ways with someone, whether amicably or not, can be an act of self-love and liberation, freeing you to welcome new, fulfilling connections into your life.

"When It's Over" is a testament to the limitless possibilities of growth and renewal. It reminds us that endings are not failures, but rather opportunities for new beginnings. It encourages us to embrace the uncomfortable spaces of uncertainty and change, knowing that they hold the keys to personal transformation.

As you turn the pages of this book, let yourself be immersed in its pages. Allow the stories, advice, and wisdom to seep into your soul. Embrace the emotions that may surface, for they are the stepping stones towards healing and growth. Through every twist and turn, remember that you are not alone in this journey. The experiences shared within these chapters are a testament to the shared human experience and the universal quest for fulfillment and happiness.

So, dear reader, let us embark on this enchanting voyage together. Let us navigate the labyrinth of emotions and emerge on the other side, stronger, wiser, and ready to embrace a future filled with authentic connections and boundless love.

1

∽

Recognizing the Signs

#1 Trust Erosion

The erosion of trust had a profound impact on our overall dynamic. Our once strong and unbreakable bond became strained, with interactions filled with tension and awkward silences. Communication became difficult, as we second-guessed everything and dissected words and actions for hidden meanings. Our relationship felt like a puzzle that we were constantly trying to solve, searching for evidence to prove or disprove our suspicions.

But the effects of trust erosion went beyond just our interactions. It took a toll on our emotional well-being. The joy we once shared seemed distant, overshadowed by the constant doubt and uncertainty. Laughter turned into hesitation, and intimacy became guarded and hesitant. We no longer felt like a united front, but rather two individuals lost in a maze of suspicion and mistrust.

Perhaps the most painful effect of trust erosion was the toll it took on our self-worth. Doubts filled the spaces once occupied by confidence and security, leaving us questioning our own value in the relationship. Each missed call or unexplained absence felt like a direct blow to our hearts, a reminder that we were no longer each other's first priority. Our self-esteem crumbled under the weight of uncertainty, leaving us feeling inadequate and unworthy of love.

Yet, amidst the chaos and despair, a glimmer of hope flickered within us. We knew deep down that we couldn't let this erosion of trust define our relationship. We were determined to find a way to rebuild what was lost, to restore the foundation of trust that once held us together.

With newfound determination, we embarked on a journey of redemption. We acknowledged our mistakes, taking ownership of the actions that contributed to the erosion. And then, we made a conscious effort to change.

We committed ourselves to open and honest communication, placing a premium on vulnerability and transparency. No longer would we hide behind veiled words or symbolic gestures; instead, we bared our souls, sharing our fears and insecurities with unwavering honesty. It was through this rawness that we started to rebuild the bridges of trust that had crumbled.

We sought guidance and support, recognizing that sometimes it takes an outside perspective to heal wounds that were self-inflicted. Together, we attended couples therapy, allowing a neutral third party to guide us towards understanding and forgiveness. Through these sessions, we learned to listen, truly listen, to one another's concerns and needs. We discovered that even the smallest gestures of support and affirmation could have a profound impact on rebuilding trust.

Time became our ally as we worked diligently to rebuild trust brick by brick. We understood that trust is not built overnight but is a continual process that requires patience and commitment. It required us to demonstrate, consistently, that our actions matched our words. It required us to truly see one another, to embrace forgiveness and move beyond past hurts.

Slowly but surely, the tension dissipated, replaced by a newfound sense of security and love. Laughter once again filled the air, and intimacy bloomed with renewed passion and vulnerability. We realized that we were not lost in a maze of suspicion, but rather on a shared path towards healing and growth.

As the days turned into weeks, and the weeks into months, our relationship transformed into something stronger and more resilient than ever before. The erosion of trust had, in its own unexpected way, become the catalyst for a deeper connection, a relationship that was now fortified by the foundation of trust we had rebuilt together.

Emerging from the depths of mistrust, we embraced a love that had been tempered by resilience and understanding. Our shattered self-worth began to mend as we realized that love is not synonymous with perfection, but rather a catalyst for growth and forgiveness. We ceased being defined by our past mistakes, instead becoming defined by the unyielding strength it took to restore what was broken.

With each sunrise, we celebrated the beauty of second chances, cherishing the new beginning that had blossomed from the ashes of our pain. Our love became an anthem of resilience, a testament to the power of forgiveness and the capacity for growth that lies within us all.

No longer burdened by the fear of betrayal, we embraced vulnerability wholeheartedly. Our hearts opened wider, allowing love to flow freely and unconditionally. We reveled in the joy of sharing our dreams, aspirations, and fears, knowing that together we could weather any storm.

In this renewed love, we found solace and strength. We became each other's safe haven, a harbor of acceptance and support. We learned to navigate the ebb and flow of life's challenges, holding onto each other with unwavering determination. No setback was insurmountable, for we knew that as long as our hearts beat in unison, we could conquer anything.

As the years passed, our love deepened and matured, reflecting the wisdom gained from our shared journey of healing. We became beacons of hope for others, inspiring them to believe in the transformative power of love and forgiveness. Our story became a testament to the resilience of the human spirit, a narrative of triumph born from the depths of despair.

In the embrace of our love, we found the courage to pursue our dreams and face our demons. We encouraged each other to step outside our comfort zones, to grow and evolve individually while remaining deeply connected. Our love became a catalyst for personal growth, a constant reminder that we were capable of achieving greatness both as individuals and as a couple.

Together, we built a life steeped in love, compassion, and understanding. Our bond served as a refuge from the chaos of the world, a place where empathy and kindness reigned supreme. We learned that love, when nurtured with patience and understanding, could overcome any obstacle and transcend any boundaries.

Though the journey had been wrought with pain and mistrust, we emerged stronger and more compassionate than ever before. We recognized that, at the core, our love was about accepting each other's imperfections and choosing to persevere, even when the odds seemed insurmountable.

In the end, it was not the darkness of the past that defined us, but rather the unwavering commitment to growth, forgiveness, and love. We had transcended the limitations of our pain and emerged as the epitome of resilience, leaving behind a legacy that would inspire generations to come.

As we walked hand in hand, gazing at the horizon ahead, we were filled with a profound sense of gratitude. We realized that our love, once broken, had been restored to new heights, becoming an unshakeable force that would guide us through the rest of our lives.

And so, we continued on our shared path, secure in the knowledge that no trial or tribulation could ever separate us. For we had discovered the true essence of love, a force that could heal, transform, and empower. And in that realization, we became the embodiment of the world's best love story.

In the final analysis, it was apparent that the erosion of trust had not annihilated us, but rather forged a relationship that was stronger, more genuine, and ultimately, more gratifying than ever before. We stood as living proof of the extraordinary power of resilience, demonstrating that even in the face of adversity, love can overcome.

Yet, amid the darkness, a flicker of hope materialized. I recognized that despite its erosion, trust still clung to its last vestiges. And within that realization, I glimpsed the potential for reconstruction. It would be an arduous journey of vulnerability, honesty, and a shared commitment to confront the harrowing truths that had plagued our relationship. If both of us were willing to embark on this journey, there existed a chance to restore trust and establish a foundation more fortitudinous than ever.

With rejuvenated determination, I mustered the courage to approach my partner, prepared to confront the fears that had kept us apart for far too long. It would not be a simple undertaking, but deep down, I knew that our love warranted the struggle. Doubt could be vanquished by trust, and we could rebuild what had been lost.

And so, our story persisted. Day by day, we confronted the unknown in tandem, holding each other's hands, armed with an enlightened comprehension of the indispensability of trust. It became a journey of growth, forgiveness, and second chances. Although our relationship had been tested, it had also been irrevocably transformed. Our love became a testament to resilience, exhibiting the indomitable power of trust and the boundless potential for redemption.

As I concluded this subchapter, a sensation of hope surged within me, setting the stage for our future. The pages continued to turn, unveiling a path laden with optimism and the revitalized bedrock of trust. Indeed, the erosion had instilled substantial agony, yet concurrently paved the way for an unyielding, more unassailable love. As we embarked on this shared odyssey, I grasped the eternal change our relationship had undergone through the trials we had withstood.

#2 Communication Breakdown

When I first met my partner, Ava, communication seemed effortless. We shared our deepest fears, dreams, and desires without hesitation. Our conversations flowed like a meandering river, carrying us closer together with each word spoken. But as time went on, the once seamless stream morphed into a turbulent current, full of misinterpretations and unspoken words.

It started with simple miscommunications - misunderstandings easily brushed off with a laugh or a gentle correction. But these hiccups gradually escalated into a pattern, pulling at the threads that once bound us so tightly. The more we struggled to communicate effectively, the further apart we drifted.

At first, I attributed the breakdown to the natural ebb and flow of any relationship. After all, it's impossible for two individuals to be in sync all the time, right? But as the miscommunications compounded, I realized the damaging effect they had on our connection. We were no longer speaking the same language, both figuratively and literally.

The impact of ineffective communication cannot be understated. It creates a breeding ground for resentment and frustration, as even the simplest of requests get lost in translation. Suddenly, every word becomes loaded with hidden meanings, and innocent conversations become battlefields. Our once flourishing connection withered away, replaced by a wall of silence and misunderstanding.

Desperate to salvage what remained of our love, we sought guidance from couples therapy. Walking into the therapist's office felt like stepping into a foreign land, unsure of the language spoken or the customs followed. But we were determined to bridge the ever-widening gap between us, to find a way back to the effortless communication we once knew.

With the guidance of our therapist, we started taking small steps towards rebuilding our connection. We learned to listen not just with our ears, but with our whole being - to truly understand the emotions and intentions behind each word. We practiced empathy, putting ourselves in each other's shoes to grasp the perspective from which our words were spoken. And most importantly, we began to communicate openly and honestly, holding nothing back in fear of being misunderstood.

As we unraveled the layers of miscommunication, we discovered the root causes beneath it all. Unresolved conflicts, unspoken expectations, and deep-seated fears that had been festering silently for far too long. It was as if the current had been churning underneath the surface, eroding the foundation of our once solid connection.

It wasn't easy. It required patience, vulnerability, and a willingness to confront our own shortcomings. But with every therapy session, the rough waters gradually calmed, and the river of communication began to flow once more. We learned new ways to express ourselves, to articulate our needs and desires in a way that the other could truly understand.

As we rebuilt our communication, we also rebuilt our trust. We realized that effective communication requires not just speaking honestly, but actively listening and validating each other's feelings. We acknowledged our own mistakes and acknowledged that we both played a part in the breakdown of our connection.

Over time, our relationship transformed. The turbulent current became a gentle stream, carrying us towards a deeper understanding and a renewed sense of intimacy. We no longer feared the miscommunications that once haunted us, but instead saw them as opportunities for growth and understanding.

Today, Ava and I are proof that even the most troubled waters can be navigated with love, patience, and a commitment to open and honest communication. We cherish the lessons we learned along the way, knowing that our journey towards reconnecting will forever strengthen the foundation of our love.

In the end, it wasn't just our relationship that benefited from our newfound communication skills - our entire lives were enriched. Our friendships, our work interactions, and even our relationship with ourselves blossomed with the power of clear and authentic expression.

As we continue to traverse the ever-changing currents of life, we hold onto the lessons we learned, knowing that effective communication remains the lifeline that will keep us connected and thriving. We are no longer victims of miscommunication but pioneers, equipped with the tools necessary to forge a path of understanding and love.

Recognizing the signs of a communication breakdown is crucial in salvaging a relationship. Misinterpretation, constant arguments, and an overall feeling of being misunderstood are all indicators that something is amiss. In my case, the turning point came when silence, rather than conversation, became the norm.

Addressing the issue required an honest evaluation of our communication patterns. It meant setting aside our egos and acknowledging our shortcomings. We had to confront our fears and insecurities, and work towards creating a safe space where open dialogue could thrive once again.

Guidance is crucial when navigating the murky waters of communication breakdown. Seeking the help of a therapist or relationship counselor can provide much-needed insight into underlying issues and offer practical tools for improvement. Additionally, practicing active listening and validation can help bridge the gap between partners, fostering understanding and empathy.

Through this process, Ava and I discovered the power of active listening. We began to prioritize truly hearing each other's thoughts and feelings, rather than simply waiting for our turn to speak. We learned to validate each other's emotions, understanding that validation does not mean agreement, but rather a genuine recognition and acceptance of the other person's experiences.

Furthermore, we started to incorporate regular check-ins into our daily lives. These intentional moments allowed us to share our thoughts, concerns, and dreams, while also ensuring that we remained on the same page. We implemented a "no judgment" rule during these conversations, creating a safe space where vulnerable thoughts could be shared without fear of criticism.

As our communication skills strengthened, we also became more attuned to non-verbal cues. We learned to read each other's body language and subtle gestures, gaining a deeper understanding of unspoken emotions and needs. This non-verbal communication became an essential part of our connection, enhancing our ability to support and comfort each other.

Along the way, we discovered the importance of self-reflection. It became clear that effective communication starts from within. We each took responsibility for our own emotions and reactions, recognizing that healthy communication required us to be in touch with ourselves. We learned to express our needs and boundaries with clarity and kindness, creating a strong foundation of self-awareness within our relationship.

As we now stand on the other side of our communication struggles, we can confidently say that our love has grown even stronger. We no longer take our connection for granted, understanding that it requires continuous effort and attention. Through our commitment to open and honest communication, we have deepened our love, trust, and understanding of one another.

In a world where miscommunication can easily lead to heartache and misunderstandings, we have become advocates for effective communication. We share our story, not to boast about our triumph over adversity, but to inspire others to face their own communication challenges head-on. We believe that every relationship has the potential to thrive when effective communication becomes a priority.

Today, Ava and I are no longer just two individuals navigating troubled waters, but a unified force that can weather any storm. With love as our compass and open communication as our guide, we are confident that our future will be filled with a love that is deep, authentic, and everlasting.

It took time and effort, but slowly we began to rebuild what had been lost. Open communication became our life raft, keeping us afloat amidst the turbulent currents. Each day brought new challenges, but the willingness to communicate and the commitment to understanding allowed us to overcome them together.

In conclusion, the breakdown of communication is a red flag in any relationship. It is a sign that the once sturdy foundation may be crumbling, and requires immediate attention and dedication to repair. By recognizing the signs, seeking guidance, and committing to open and honest communication, couples can navigate the treacherous waters and emerge stronger on the other side.

#3 Emotional Disconnect

In the beginning, everything seemed perfect. The way her eyes sparkled when she laughed, the warmth of her touch, and the way her words resonated deep within my soul – it all created an unbreakable emotional connection. It was as if we were two puzzle pieces, fitting seamlessly together, completing each other in ways words could never express.

But as time passed, the spark started to fade. The laughter became forced, the touch became distant, and the words lost their impact. It was in these moments that I realized something was missing, something crucial to the survival of our relationship – the emotional connection. Like an anchor weighing us down, its absence left a void, an emptiness that could no longer be ignored.

Emotional connection is the foundation upon which all relationships are built. It goes beyond mere physical attraction or shared interests; it is the deep understanding and empathy that binds two souls together. It is the ability to not only listen but to truly hear, to not only see but to truly understand, and to not only touch but to truly feel.

Without this emotional bond, relationships become empty shells, mere facades of what they once were. It is through emotional connection that we derive meaning, fulfillment, and intimacy in our connections with others. It is this connection that forms the bedrock of trust, vulnerability, and authentic love.

When the emotional connection begins to wane, it is a sign that something in the relationship is amiss. It is not simply a passing phase or a temporary rough patch. It is a clear indication that change is needed, that the foundation upon which the relationship was built has become cracked, and that it must either be repaired or rebuilt entirely.

The absence of emotional connection can manifest in various ways. It may be a lack of communication – conversations becoming shallow and unfulfilling, with words spoken but never heard. It may be a lack of intimacy – physical touch devoid of passion, devoid of emotion. Or it may be a lack of understanding – the ability to empathize and truly see one another disappearing, replaced by indifference and a growing divide.

In these moments of realization, it is essential to confront the issue head-on. Pretending that everything is fine will only prolong the inevitable, allowing the distance between hearts to grow wider and the love that once flourished to wither away completely.

Rebuilding the emotional connection requires effort from both parties involved. It demands open and honest communication, a willingness to be vulnerable, and a genuine desire to understand and rekindle what has been lost. It means setting aside time to connect on a deeper level, to engage in meaningful conversations, and to actively listen to one another's thoughts and feelings.

It also entails rediscovering the unique qualities and quirks that drew you to each other in the first place. Whether it is through shared hobbies, adventures, or simply quality time spent together, finding ways to reconnect and create new memories can reignite the flame that was once so bright.

But perhaps most crucially, rebuilding the emotional connection requires self-reflection and introspection. It demands a willingness to examine one's own actions and behaviors, to acknowledge any role played in the deterioration of the bond, and to take responsibility for making positive changes. It is only through personal growth and self-improvement that true transformation can occur.

Rebuilding an emotional connection requires patience, understanding, and a commitment to the journey ahead. It is not a quick fix or a one-time effort, but a continuous process that requires ongoing nurturing and care. It may take time to heal old wounds, to build trust anew, and to rediscover the depth of love that once existed. But with dedication and perseverance, it is possible to breathe life back into a dying connection and create a love that is not only enduring but thriving.

In the end, the strength of a relationship lies not in its absence of challenges, but in its ability to overcome them. By recognizing the significance of emotional connection and actively working to restore it when it falters, we can create a love story that transcends mere perfection and becomes an enduring tale of growth, resilience, and unwavering love.

The road to reconnecting emotionally is not an easy one. It requires honest introspection, open communication, and a willingness to confront the underlying issues that have contributed to the disconnect. But if both parties are willing to invest the time, effort, and vulnerability required, the emotional connection can be rediscovered, rekindled, and ultimately strengthened.

Love is a journey, and like any journey, there will be twists and turns, obstacles and detours. But it is through these hardships that we grow and evolve both as individuals and as partners. Through the exploration of our emotional disconnect, we can learn valuable lessons about ourselves and our needs, paving the way for a more fulfilling and authentic connection with others.

As we navigate the winding path towards rebuilding our emotional connection, we must remember to approach each step with compassion and understanding. It is essential to give each other the space to express our emotions and concerns without judgment, creating a safe and nurturing environment for open and honest communication.

In this journey, we may uncover aspects of ourselves that need healing or areas where we have contributed to the disconnection. It is crucial to take responsibility for our actions and actively work towards personal growth. By showing accountability and making necessary changes, we demonstrate our commitment to not only restoring the emotional bond but also creating a healthier and more harmonious relationship.

Lost connections are not only rebuilt through words but through actions as well. Small gestures of love, kindness, and appreciation go a long way in reigniting the spark that once existed between us. We must be mindful of each other's needs and make a conscious effort to meet them, allowing our actions to be a reflection of the love and care we have for one another.

As we continue on this journey, it is vital to keep our expectations in check and embrace the ebb and flow of progress. Some days may feel like breakthroughs, while others may feel like setbacks. It is during these moments of discouragement that we must remember the commitment we made to ourselves and each other. We must stand together, supporting and encouraging one another to keep moving forward.

Along the path of reconnecting emotionally, there will be moments of vulnerability and discomfort. It is within these moments that true growth occurs. By facing our fears, insecurities, and past wounds, we create opportunities for healing and transformation. As we share our deepest selves with each other, we build a profound level of trust and intimacy, strengthening the foundation of our connection.

In the end, the process of rebuilding an emotional connection is not about fixing what is broken but rather about creating something new and beautiful. It is an opportunity to dig deep, to not only understand one another but also to understand ourselves. Through this process, we can cultivate a love that is not stagnant, but a love that continuously evolves and deepens over time.

So let us embark on this journey together, hand in hand, with a renewed sense of hope and determination. For in the realm of love, there are infinite possibilities waiting to be uncovered. Together, we can rebuild our emotional connection and create a love story that will stand the test of time.

So, my dear reader, if you find yourself trapped in the mire of emotional disconnect, do not despair. Recognize it as an opportunity for growth, change, and ultimately, a deeper connection. For it is in the face of adversity that the true strength of a relationship is revealed, and when it's over, you will be stronger, wiser, and more capable of finding the love and connection you truly deserve.

#4 Understanding Red Flags

Firstly, a major red flag in any relationship is a lack of communication. Communication forms the foundation of a healthy connection, allowing partners to express their needs, desires, and concerns openly. When one or both partners shy away from discussing important matters or constantly avoid conversations that require vulnerability, it is a clear sign that the relationship is heading towards a dangerous territory. Disregarding the significance of communication not only limits the growth of the relationship but also leads to frustration, misunderstandings, and feelings of isolation.

Without open and honest communication, couples are unable to build trust and understanding. This lack of trust can seep into other aspects of the relationship, causing doubt, suspicions, and insecurities to arise. Unresolved issues begin to accumulate, creating a heavy and toxic atmosphere between partners.

Moreover, without proper communication, conflicts are left unresolved, simmering beneath the surface and waiting to explode. These unaddressed issues can manifest in passive-aggressive behavior, resentment, and even emotional or physical abuse. It becomes a breeding ground for constant arguments and a cycle of hurtful behavior.

Communication extends beyond just talking; it involves active listening, empathy, and respect for one another's feelings. When one partner shuts down or dismisses the other's concerns, it creates a significant barrier to working through problems together. This leads to a breakdown in connection and a growing emotional distance.

In healthy relationships, communication brings about growth and understanding. It allows couples to navigate challenges and find solutions as a team. It provides a safe space for both partners to share their vulnerabilities and create deeper intimacy.

To address the lack of communication, both partners must be willing to acknowledge its importance and commit to improving it. This requires being present and attentive during conversations, practicing active listening, and validating each other's experiences. It also involves setting aside time to engage in open dialogue, free from distractions or defensiveness.

Seeking professional help, such as couples therapy, can also be beneficial. A trained therapist can guide partners in developing effective communication strategies and resolving deep-seated issues that hinder connection.

Remember, a healthy relationship thrives on open and honest communication. It is the very foundation upon which love, trust, and intimacy can flourish. By prioritizing communication, couples can overcome obstacles together, strengthen their bond, and create a lasting and fulfilling partnership.

Another red flag is a significant power imbalance within the relationship. Relationships should be built on equality, respect, and shared decision-making. However, when one partner consistently dominates the decision-making process, dismisses the opinions of the other, or belittles their ideas, it indicates a power imbalance that can be detrimental to the long-term health and happiness of the relationship. Such imbalances can lead to feelings of inadequacy, resentment, and further perpetuate a toxic dynamic.

Additionally, toxic relationships often exhibit signs of emotional or physical abuse. This can manifest in various ways, such as constant criticism, insults, threats, or even physical violence. Relationships should always be built on a foundation of love, trust, and support, not fear and intimidation. No one deserves to be mistreated or live in constant fear of their partner's actions. Recognizing and addressing the presence of any form of abuse is crucial for one's physical and emotional well-being.

Furthermore, a lack of trust in a relationship is a clear indicator of toxicity. Trust is the bedrock upon which a strong partnership is built. It involves having faith in each other's intentions, actions, and words. When trust is absent or consistently broken, it creates an atmosphere of doubt, suspicion, and insecurity. Without trust, it becomes challenging for a relationship to thrive, as doubts and insecurities fester and erode the foundation of love and connection.

Jealousy and a lack of trust can be destructive to a relationship and should be addressed promptly. Trust is the foundation of a healthy partnership, and without it, doubt and suspicion will erode the connection between partners. In a healthy relationship, both partners give each other the benefit of the doubt and have faith in each other's loyalty.

Constant jealousy, accompanied by accusations and a need for control, indicates deeper issues within the relationship. It often stems from insecurity and can quickly transform the dynamics into a toxic environment. It is essential to address jealousy openly and honestly, exploring the root causes and working together to rebuild trust.

Moreover, a healthy relationship values individuality and the freedom to pursue personal interests and goals. It is crucial to encourage and support each other's growth, allowing each person to bring their unique qualities and passions into the relationship. Losing oneself in a relationship and sacrificing personal fulfillment is not healthy or sustainable in the long run.

Lastly, empathy and compassion are vital components of a healthy relationship. Partners must be able to understand and share in each other's emotions, practicing active listening and validating each other's experiences. In a toxic relationship, one or both partners may consistently dismiss or invalidate the other's feelings, leading to emotional hurt and distance.

In summary, a healthy relationship prioritizes trust, individuality, and empathy. It requires open communication, mutual support, and a commitment to personal growth. Recognizing and addressing the warning signs of jealousy, a lack of trust, and a lack of empathy is crucial for the well-being and happiness of both partners. Building a healthy relationship takes effort and a willingness to confront and resolve issues as they arise, creating a strong and fulfilling partnership.

Addressing jealousy and building trust requires open and honest communication. Both partners must be willing to discuss their insecurities and fears without judgment. This may involve therapy or counseling to dig deeper into the root causes of jealousy and work toward healing and overcoming these negative emotions.

Additionally, a healthy relationship requires space and independence. Each partner should feel free to pursue their own interests, maintain their own friendships, and have moments of solitude. This not only promotes personal growth but also prevents codependency, which can lead to a lack of individuality and suffocation within the relationship.

Furthermore, a healthy relationship involves mutual respect and the absence of any form of abuse, be it physical, emotional, or verbal. It is crucial to establish boundaries and ensure that they are respected by both partners. Any violation of these boundaries should be taken seriously and addressed promptly, seeking professional help if necessary.

Moreover, forgiveness is an essential aspect of any healthy relationship. Mistakes and disagreements are inevitable, but holding onto grudges and refusing to forgive can poison the relationship. Forgiveness allows for growth, understanding, and the rebuilding of trust, creating a stronger foundation for the future.

Finally, prioritizing quality time together is crucial. In the hustle and bustle of daily life, it is important for partners to dedicate time solely to each other, away from distractions. This can be as simple as a romantic walk, a date night, or even a weekend getaway. Nurture the connection and keep the flame of love alive by actively investing in the relationship.

In summary, a healthy relationship is built on open communication, trust, respect, independence, forgiveness, and quality time together. It requires constant effort, understanding, and a commitment to growth. By recognizing and addressing the warning signs of toxicity, fostering trust and understanding, and prioritizing each other's well-being, couples can create a loving and fulfilling relationship that stands the test of time.

Recognizing these red flags in a relationship is vital for one's personal growth and emotional well-being. It is essential to address these concerns early on and navigate them through open and honest communication. Ultimately, staying in a toxic or unhealthy relationship can be detrimental to one's mental health, happiness, and overall self-worth. By acknowledging the warning signs and taking the necessary steps to address them, individuals can save themselves from undue pain and find the healthy and fulfilling relationships they deserve.

#5 Intuition and Gut Feelings

As humans, we are endowed with a remarkable tool - our intuition. It is that elusive but undeniable feeling that nudges us in a certain direction, whispering softly amidst the noise of our thoughts. Intuition is often overlooked or dismissed as irrational, but it holds a deep wisdom that can guide us through complex situations, especially in matters of the heart.

When it comes to relationships, our intuition can be a powerful ally in helping us recognize when it's time to let go. It is this unfathomable, yet unmistakable gut feeling that leads us to the realization that the connection we once cherished has withered away. Our intuitive sense, honed through experiences and self-reflection, becomes a compass guiding us towards what is truly aligned with our happiness.

In the early stages of a relationship, intuition manifests as a delicate whisper, expressing its approval or urging caution. It becomes an integral part of our decision-making process, gently prodding our hearts when the compatibility fades away. We may begin to notice subtle changes, a growing discomfort, or a nagging feeling deep within. These signs, often dismissed as minor inconveniences, are the early whispers of intuition, illuminating the path ahead.

However, in the midst of the chaos of emotions, it can be difficult to discern between intuition and fear. We find ourselves grappling with doubts, second-guessing our instincts, and ignoring that familiar twinge in our gut. We are plagued by the what-ifs, clinging to the hope that things will improve, afraid to face the potential pain of letting go. It is at these crossroads that we must learn to lean into our intuition, trusting its wisdom to guide us towards the truth.

For it is intuition that holds the key to our liberation, urging us to embrace the transformative power of vulnerability and release ourselves from the chains of stagnant relationships. It is through intuition that we find the strength to confront our fears, to confront the unknown, and to open ourselves up to the possibility of greater love and fulfillment.

As we cultivate a deeper connection with our intuition, we begin to recognize the patterns and red flags that we may have previously overlooked. We learn to trust the whispers from within, no matter how faint they may be, for they carry with them the wisdom of our authentic selves. Our intuition becomes a beacon of trust, guiding us away from toxic dynamics and towards relationships that honor our worth and nourish our growth.

But let us not forget, dear reader, that intuition is not only a tool for recognizing when it's time to let go. It is also a compass that leads us towards the possibilities of new beginnings. It stirs our souls, igniting a spark of curiosity and desire for change. It nudges us towards connections that are filled with passion, understanding, and an unwavering sense of alignment.

In matters of the heart, intuition is not a luxury, but a necessity. It is the voice that speaks from our deepest core, reminding us of our inherent worthiness of love and happiness. It is an unwavering guide, helping us navigate the complexities and uncertainties of human connection.

So, my dear reader, I implore you to listen. Listen to the whispers of your intuition, for they carry the wisdom of your heart. Trust in its guidance as you navigate the ever-evolving tapestry of relationships. And with each step, remember that your intuition is not only a tool but a gift bestowed upon you, a testament to your inherent ability to navigate the twisting paths of love and find your way back to the truth of who you are.

To tap into our inner wisdom, we must embark on a journey of self-discovery. By fostering self-awareness and cultivating a deep connection with our feelings, we can better discern the messages of our intuition.

This involves quieting the noise around us, creating space for introspection, and listening attentively to the whispers of our souls.

Journaling can be a powerful tool in this process. Writing down our thoughts, emotions, and observations provides a tangible medium through which our intuition can speak to us. By reflecting on our journal entries, we can uncover patterns, identify recurring doubts, and gain clarity on the state of our relationship. This practice allows us to access the deeper wisdom within us, enabling us to make informed decisions based on what truly resonates with our core values and desires.

Additionally, seeking the counsel of trusted loved ones can provide valuable insights. Sharing our experiences with those who know us well can shed light on blind spots we may have overlooked. Their objective perspective can help us navigate the labyrinth of emotions, providing clarity and support as we explore the path ahead.

As we embark on this journey, it is important to remember that our intuition is not infallible. It is influenced by our past experiences, fears, and desires. Therefore, it is crucial to approach our intuition with discernment and self-awareness. We must question, reflect, and challenge our own assumptions to ensure that our intuition is guiding us towards healthy and fulfilling relationships.

Sometimes, our intuition may lead us to make difficult choices. It may prompt us to walk away from a relationship that no longer serves us or confront challenging truths about ourselves or our partner. These moments require courage and resilience. But by honoring our intuition, we are honoring the deepest parts of ourselves and embracing the potential for growth and transformation.

Above all, in matters of the heart, we must remember to be gentle with ourselves. We are human, and we are bound to make mistakes along the way. We may misinterpret the messages of our intuition or be swayed by external pressures. But even when things don't go as planned, our intuition remains a steadfast guide, always leading us back to our own truth and the love we are worthy of.

So, my dear reader, I encourage you to embark on this journey of self-discovery and listen to the whispers of your intuition. Trust in its guidance, question, reflect, and be gentle with yourself along the way. In matters of the heart, intuition is not just a luxury; it is a necessity. Embrace it, honor it, and let it lead you towards the love and happiness you deserve.

In recognizing when a relationship has run its course, we must learn to trust our intuition and gut feelings. By developing a strong connection with our inner selves, cultivating self-awareness, and seeking guidance from those who hold our best interests at heart, we can make informed decisions. Intuition becomes our guide, leading us toward authentic connections and a future filled with love and fulfillment.

2

∽

Navigating Friendships

Growing Apart

As I sat down to write this subchapter, my mind wandered back in time to countless memories of friendships that had once meant the world to me. People whom I considered family, confidantes, and partners-in-crime. Yet, despite the strength of our connection at one point, life had a cunning way of leading us down different paths. This subchapter explores the bittersweet process of growing apart in friendships, acknowledging the factors that contribute to this shift and offering guidance on how to navigate it with compassion.

In the world of friendship, growing apart is as natural as the ebb and flow of the tides. Just as we evolve as individuals, so too do our relationships. It is essential to remember that this divergence should not be viewed as a personal failure or a sign that something is inherently wrong with the friendship. Instead, it is a testament to the growth and change each of us undergoes during our journey through life. Recognizing that growing apart is a common occurrence provides the foundation to approach this shift with empathy and understanding.

The first factor that contributes to growing apart is the changes that occur within ourselves. As we embark on personal journeys of self-discovery, we may find our values, interests, and priorities shifting. Our needs and aspirations evolve, propelling us towards new experiences and opportunities. This interplay between personal growth and friendship sets the stage for the natural divergence that often arises.

Additionally, external circumstances can shape the direction of a friendship. Life's demands such as work commitments, geographical relocations, and the formation of new relationships can lead to a reduction in the time and energy we can invest in our existing friendships. It is crucial to acknowledge the impact these external factors have on each individual, appreciating that their inability to devote sufficient time to the friendship is not a reflection of their feelings or importance as a friend.

Navigating the process of growing apart in friendship requires a delicate balance of introspection and communication. The first step is to take the time to reflect on your own growth and changes. Ask yourself what you truly value in a friendship and whether those values align with the current state of the relationship. This reflection will help you gain clarity and determine whether it is a temporary phase or a signal for a more significant shift.

When you feel ready to address the situation, it is essential to approach the conversation with empathy and understanding. Choose a comfortable and neutral setting where you both can openly express your thoughts and feelings. Start by acknowledging the changes you have both experienced and how they may have affected the friendship. Share your own reflections and emotions, and encourage your friend to do the same.

During this conversation, it is crucial to maintain an open mind and to listen without judgment. Remember that growing apart does not mean the friendship is over or that your bond no longer holds value. It simply means that both parties are evolving into different versions of themselves. Be willing to explore ways to adapt the friendship to accommodate this growth or consider the possibility of transitioning into a different type of relationship, such as being acquaintances or supportive from a distance.

Ultimately, growing apart in friendship can be a challenging and emotional process, but it can also be an opportunity for personal growth and understanding. By navigating this shift with compassion and communicating openly, we can honor the memories and lessons shared while embracing the changes that life presents. After all, the true mark of a strong friendship is not solely in its longevity but in the love and support shared, regardless of the paths we choose to walk.

While growing apart is an organic process, navigating it with compassion is essential for both parties involved. This starts with open and honest communication. Expressing our thoughts, emotions, and evolving needs can foster understanding and provide an opportunity for mutual growth, even if it means acknowledging that the friendship may need to take a different form.

It is crucial to approach this conversation with sensitivity and empathy. Instead of blaming or making assumptions, focus on expressing your own feelings and concerns. This can create a safe space for the other person to share their own perspective, fostering a deeper understanding between both parties. Remember, this is not about finding fault or placing blame but rather about acknowledging the changes that have naturally occurred.

In doing so, we honor the memories and lessons shared throughout the course of the friendship. Reflecting on the joyous moments, the growth we experienced together, and the support we offered one another can help us appreciate the value that the friendship brought into our lives. It reminds us that even if we may be taking different paths now, the connection we once had was meaningful and shaped us into the individuals we are today.

As we navigate the changes that life presents, we must also embrace the concept of personal growth. Recognize that it is natural for individuals to change and evolve over time. Our interests, priorities, and goals may shift, leading us down different avenues. This in no way diminishes the love and support that once existed. Rather, it allows us to explore new aspects of ourselves and carve out our own paths.

Embracing this growth while also acknowledging the changes in the friendship does not mean that we have to completely sever ties. It may simply mean that the dynamic of the relationship adjusts, allowing for new connections and perspectives to form. This understanding opens the door to a broader network of support, nurtures our own personal development, and creates space for new friendships to blossom.

Ultimately, the measure of a strong friendship lies not solely in its longevity, but in the love and support shared, regardless of the different paths we choose to walk. By navigating the growing apart process with compassion, communication, and understanding, we can honor the essence of the friendship while allowing ourselves and the other person the freedom to explore and thrive.

So, let us approach the changing tides of friendship with grace, acceptance, and gratitude. Let us cherish the memories shared and embrace the lessons learned, knowing that the strength of a friendship lies not in its eternal presence, but in the impact it has on our lives.

Sometimes, despite our best efforts, the natural trajectory of a friendship leads us down separate paths. While the prospect of letting go can be daunting, it is essential to recognize that this does not diminish the value or significance of the experience shared. Sometimes, growing apart is necessary for both individuals to continue thriving in their respective journeys, allowing room for new relationships and opportunities to flourish.

As I reflect on my own experiences, I have come to appreciate the beauty in growing apart. While it can be painful and require a period of adjustment, it opens the door to new connections, discoveries, and personal growth. Navigating this process with compassion enables us to honor the memories, cherish the growth, and celebrate the friendship we once had, even as we continue down our separate paths.

In conclusion, growing apart is a natural process within friendships and should not be seen as a failure or a reflection of personal worth. By understanding the factors that contribute to this shift and approaching it with compassion, we can honor the growth and change both within ourselves and our friends. Ultimately, navigating this shift allows us to move forward with gratitude, cherishing the memories, and embracing the new friendships that lie ahead.

Toxic Friendships

Step 1: Recognizing Toxic Friendships

As I sat in my dimly lit room, surrounded by old journals filled with memories of laughter and shared adventures, I couldn't ignore the heavy weight in my heart. It was the weight of toxicity that had slowly seeped into my relationships, poisoning them from within. Toxic friendships, like mold growing silently in the dark corners of our lives, can be hard to recognize at first.

To begin the journey of self-awareness, it is crucial to understand the subtle signs that indicate a toxic friendship. Patterns of negativity and constant criticism, whether directed at you or others, are clear indicators of toxicity. In these friendships, there is no warmth or genuine support, only a superficial façade that crumbles under scrutiny. Words that were once laced with kindness now pierce through your heart like a dagger, leaving scars that deepen with every encounter.

But recognizing toxicity is just the first step; the real challenge lies in freeing oneself from its clutches. It requires strength, courage, and an unwavering belief in one's own worth. As I sifted through those old journals, I stumbled upon forgotten pages that held fragments of confidence and self-assurance. It was a reminder that I was once capable of flourishing within healthy relationships, and I could be again.

With newfound determination, I set out on a path of self-discovery. I immersed myself in books that spoke of self-love and self-care, seeking guidance from the minds of those who had traveled this road before me. Each page turned was like a beacon of hope, illuminating the way forward amidst the darkness. I allowed the words of wisdom to seep into my soul, nurturing it and reminding it of the love and respect it deserved.

As I grew more aware of the toxicity that had tainted my past, I also became acutely aware of the energy I allowed into my life. I no longer had room for negativity; my space was reserved for those who uplifted and cherished me. It wasn't easy to let go of friendships that had once held such significance, but I knew that in order to grow, I had to sever the ties that bound me to the shadows of my past.

And so, one by one, I bid farewell to those who had caused me pain. It was a bittersweet goodbye, for in letting go, I released not only the toxicity but also the memories of shared laughter and adventures. But I understood that those memories were tinged with a darkness that obscured their true beauty. It was time to make space for new connections, ones that would nurture my growth and bring genuine joy into my life.

As the days turned into weeks and the weeks into months, I basked in the lightness that came with shedding toxic friendships. I laughed louder, loved deeper, and discovered a newfound sense of freedom. Every day was a reminder that I was deserving of healthy relationships, ones that would uplift and inspire me to be the best version of myself.

In the quiet solitude of my dimly lit room, with those old journals closed and tucked away, I knew I had embarked on a journey of self-empowerment. No longer was I defined by the toxic friendships that once held me captive; I was now the author of my own narrative. And with every word penned, I embraced my role as the world's best writer – the writer of my own story, filled with love, growth, and the power to inspire others to break free from the toxicity that stifles their souls.

Step 2: The Detrimental Effects

Toxic friendships, like a venomous snake, inject poison into our lives, slowly eroding our self-esteem and confidence. It becomes harder to trust our own judgment, as every decision is met with criticism or belittlement. We find ourselves constantly seeking approval and validation from someone who should be a source of comfort and support.

Over time, the effects of these toxic relationships can seep into other areas of our lives, poisoning our overall well-being. Our mental health deteriorates as we internalize the negativity, leaving us questioning our worth and value. Physically, the stress and anxiety caused by these friendships can manifest in various ways, from sleepless nights to chronic headaches, robbing us of the energy we need to thrive.

But there comes a time when we must recognize the toxicity for what it is, and make the decision to break free from its suffocating grip. It is not an easy choice, for we have grown accustomed to the familiarity, despite its toxicity. However, we must remember that our happiness and well-being should never be compromised for the sake of a friendship that brings us only pain.

With each step we take towards liberation, we begin to rediscover ourselves. We learn to trust our instincts and regain the confidence that was chipped away by the venomous words and actions of our former friend. We surround ourselves with positive influences, those who lift us up and encourage our growth, instead of dragging us down into the depths of despair.

As we distance ourselves from toxic friendships, we find solace in our own company, embracing the freedom and autonomy that comes from not relying on someone else's approval. Slowly but surely, we untangle ourselves from the web of negativity that once enveloped us, reclaiming our sense of self and becoming architects of our own happiness.

In this process of healing, we must also forgive ourselves for allowing toxic friendships to infiltrate our lives. Without blame or judgment, we acknowledge that no one is immune to the allure of toxic relationships. We recognize that it is our strength and resilience that guides us towards healthier connections.

As time passes, we begin to witness the beauty that arises from shedding the weight of toxicity. Our mental and physical health start to flourish, and we discover a newfound clarity of mind. The sleepless nights and chronic headaches gradually dissipate, making way for positivity and a renewed zest for life.

In the absence of toxicity, we build genuine and authentic friendships, ones that nurture our growth and celebrate our individuality. We learn to set boundaries, recognizing that we deserve respect and kindness in all our relationships. We become better communicators, expressing our needs and emotions without fear of judgment or rejection.

Woven into our stories of overcoming toxic friendships is the realization that we are deserving and capable of healthy, uplifting connections. We become the authors of our own narratives, crafting a life enriched by genuine friendships and boundless self-love.

And perhaps, in sharing our experiences, we can inspire others who are trapped in the throes of toxic friendships to find the courage to break free and embrace the beautiful, fulfilling relationships that await them. For in the end, it is only through the power of self-love and the strength to let go that we can truly flourish in the garden of life.

Step 3: Disengaging from Toxic Friendships

Recognizing toxicity in a friendship is the first courageous step towards freeing ourselves from its suffocating grip. It is essential to release ourselves from the chains that keep us bound to unhealthy connections, even in the face of fear and uncertainty.

While it may be tempting to confront the toxic friend and demand explanations for their behavior, it is often more empowering to disengage without providing the toxic individual with the opportunity to manipulate or hurt us further. Building strong boundaries and limiting contact allows us to regain control over our own lives and protect ourselves from further harm.

Seeking support from trusted loved ones and professional counselors can provide invaluable guidance and validation during this challenging process. Surrounding ourselves with a network of genuine, nurturing relationships can cultivate a sense of healing and empowerment, reaffirming our innate worth and reminding us of the beauty that lies within us.

As we venture on this path of liberation, it is crucial to redirect our energy towards self-reflection and personal growth. Examining the patterns and beliefs that led us into this toxic friendship helps us understand why we accepted such negativity in our lives. Through introspection, we uncover our vulnerabilities, address our insecurities, and begin the process of self-empowerment.

In the face of adversity, it is essential to cultivate self-compassion and forgiveness. We must recognize that we are not defined by the toxicity we endured, but rather by our resilience, courage, and capacity to heal. By embracing forgiveness, we release ourselves from the weight of bitterness and resentment, freeing our hearts to welcome love and positivity.

Moving forward, we must remain vigilant and discerning, actively safeguarding our emotional well-being from potential toxic influences. Setting clear boundaries becomes a non-negotiable aspect of our new-found self-love. We learn to say no without guilt, to prioritize our needs, and to protect our precious energy.

Yet, in this journey, we should not lose sight of the lessons we have learned. Toxic friendships, however painful, can be powerful catalysts for personal growth. Through these experiences, we become more attuned to our intuition, refining our ability to detect and avoid toxic individuals. We emerge wiser, stronger, and equipped with the knowledge to build healthier, more fulfilling relationships in the future.

As we step into the light of independence and self-worth, we embrace the joy of authentic connections. We savor the company of those who lift us up, inspire us to become our best selves, and celebrate our successes. We become intentional in nurturing mutual respect, support, and trust, forging bonds that bring happiness, fulfillment, and a renewed sense of purpose.

In freeing ourselves from the shackles of toxic friendship, we embark on a journey towards self-discovery and self-love. We become the authors of our own destiny, crafting a life filled with joy, authenticity, and genuine connections. By recognizing and breaking free from toxicity, we reclaim our power, our happiness, and our ability to create the beautiful story we deserve.

In conclusion, toxic friendships can be insidious, silently eroding our well-being over time. Recognizing these toxic patterns, understanding their detrimental effects, and disengaging with courage and self-love are essential steps towards reclaiming our happiness and restoring our sense of worthiness. By setting boundaries and seeking healthy connections, we can create a vibrant tapestry of relationships that uplift and nourish our souls, leaving no room for toxicity to breed and darken our lives. It is within our power to break free from the chains of toxic friendships and choose a path that leads to healing, growth, and genuine connection.

Setting Boundaries

In my own journey of self-discovery and personal growth, I have come to understand the significance of setting boundaries in friendships. Before, I used to believe that being a good friend meant being available at any given moment, no matter the cost to my own well-being. But over time, I realized that without clear boundaries, I was constantly feeling drained and overwhelmed.

The problem was that I was giving so much of myself to others without considering my own needs. I was constantly saying "yes" to every invitation, every favor, and every request, afraid that if I didn't, I would be seen as a selfish or ungrateful friend. I didn't want to disappoint anyone or risk damaging the friendships I cherished so deeply.

But as my emotional and physical exhaustion mounted, I started to question whether true friendship should come at such a high price. I began to realize that setting boundaries wasn't about being selfish; it was about valuing and respecting myself enough to prioritize my own well-being.

Moreover, I discovered the value of self-reflection and self-awareness. Regularly checking in with myself and assessing my emotions, energy levels, and overall well-being helped me determine when I needed to set boundaries and when I risked overextending myself.

Additionally, practicing self-compassion played a vital role in my journey. I came to understand that setting boundaries did not make me a bad friend but rather a healthier and more balanced individual who could authentically show up. Granting myself permission to prioritize self-care and my own needs became an act of self-love that ultimately strengthened my friendships.

In addition to verbal communication, I found it effective to establish boundaries through my actions. Learning to confidently say "no" without guilt, declining invitations or requests that did not align with my values or priorities, and making time for activities that brought me joy proved essential in maintaining healthy boundaries.

As I developed a strong foundation of healthy boundaries in my friendships, I noticed a significant transformation in the dynamics of these relationships. Friendships became more balanced, with a mutual respect for each other's boundaries. We were able to support and uplift one another without sacrificing our own needs.

To summarize, my journey of setting boundaries in friendships has been a profound one. It has allowed me to foster deeper connections, prioritize self-care, and build a network of relationships that nourish and support me. I have come to realize that setting boundaries is not only crucial for my own well-being but also for the health and longevity of my friendships.

Furthermore, I recognize the importance of identifying signs of unhealthy boundaries in my friendships. When someone consistently crosses my boundaries or dismisses my needs, it is a clear indication of an imbalance in the relationship. Instead of accepting such behavior, I now understand the importance of addressing it and establishing clear consequences for repeated boundary violations.

Lastly, I will provide practical techniques for self-reflection and identifying personal boundaries. Understanding my values, needs, and limits enabled me to establish more solid boundaries in my friendships. I have learned to listen to my intuition and recognize when a situation or request exceeds what is comfortable or reasonable.

In conclusion, setting boundaries in my friendships has not only improved my well-being but also created space for healthier and more fulfilling connections. I have realized that true friendship should be built on mutual respect, understanding, and support. By valuing my own needs and limitations, I have created a foundation for authentic and balanced friendships. Join me in discovering the power of setting boundaries in friendships and embarking on a journey toward healthier, more fulfilling relationships.

Another lesson I learned was the power of self-reflection and self-awareness. I prioritized regular check-ins with myself, taking the time to assess my emotions, energy levels, and overall well-being. This allowed me to better understand when I needed to set boundaries and when I was at risk of overextending myself.

I also discovered the importance of self-compassion in this journey. Setting boundaries didn't make me a bad friend; it made me a healthier, more balanced individual who could show up authentically. Giving myself permission to prioritize self-care and my needs was an act of self-love that ultimately strengthened my friendships.

In addition to communicating boundaries verbally, I found it helpful to establish clear boundaries through my actions. Learning to say "no" without guilt, declining invitations that didn't align with my values or priorities, and making time for myself and activities that brought me joy were crucial in maintaining healthy boundaries.

As I developed a strong foundation of healthy boundaries in my friendships, I noticed a significant shift in the dynamics of these relationships. Friendships became more balanced, with a mutual respect for each other's boundaries. We were able to support and uplift one another without sacrificing our own needs.

In conclusion, setting boundaries in friendships has been a transformative journey. It has allowed me to cultivate deeper connections, prioritize self-care, and build a network of relationships that nourish and support me. I have come to realize that setting boundaries is not only crucial for my own well-being but also for the health and longevity of my friendships.

Another valuable lesson I learned was recognizing the signs of unhealthy boundaries in my friendships. When one person consistently crosses my boundaries or dismisses my needs, it is a red flag indicating an imbalance in the relationship. Instead of tolerating such behavior, I now know the importance of addressing it and setting clear consequences for repeated boundary violations.

Additionally, I will provide practical techniques for self-reflection and identifying personal boundaries. Understanding my values, needs, and limits allowed me to establish more solid boundaries in my friendships. I learned to listen to my intuition and recognize when a situation or request was pushing me beyond what was comfortable or reasonable.

Lastly, I will discuss the importance of being flexible and open to evolving boundaries. Friendships are dynamic, and as we grow and change, our boundaries may need adjusting. It is crucial to regularly evaluate and re-evaluate our boundaries to ensure they align with our evolving needs and values.

By setting boundaries in my friendships, I not only improved my own well-being but also created space for healthier and more fulfilling connections. I realized that true friendship should be built on mutual respect, understanding, and support. By valuing my own needs and limitations, I was able to create a foundation for authentic and balanced friendships. Join me in discovering the power of setting boundaries in friendships, and let's embark on a journey towards healthier, more fulfilling relationships together.

Honoring Growth and Change

One of the primary challenges that arise when personal growth and change affect friendships is the fear of losing the connection that once bound us together. As we embark on our individual journeys of growth, we often find ourselves drifting apart from those who were once our closest confidantes. It can be difficult to accept that the dynamics of a friendship may need to change, especially when we value the history and memories shared with that person. The fear of losing what once was can weigh heavily on us as we grapple with the need to move on.

Yet, amidst this fear and uncertainty, there is a solution - the first step towards honoring growth and change is to accept the evolving nature of friendships. Just as the seasons change, so too do the people in our lives. Change is an inherent part of life, and it is essential that we embrace it with open hearts and minds. Recognizing that friendships are not stagnant but rather fluid will free us from the constraints of clinging to the past, and allow us to appreciate the growth that each person undergoes.

In accepting the evolving nature of friendships, we must also learn to communicate honestly and openly with our friends. It is crucial to express our feelings and intentions clearly, without fear or hesitation. When personal growth and change arise, it can be easy to assume that our friends will automatically understand why we are changing or why our priorities are shifting. However, assumptions can lead to misunderstandings and ultimately, the deterioration of friendships.

Instead, let us have the courage to have heartfelt conversations with our friends. Let us share our hopes, dreams, and aspirations, explaining how these changes are essential for our personal growth and happiness. By doing so, we can create a safe space where our friends can express their own desires for growth and change, fostering a mutual understanding and respect that will strengthen the bond between us.

It is important to note that not all friendships may survive the challenges of personal growth and change. Some relationships may naturally fade away as we move along different paths in life. And although it can be painful to realize that some friendships may come to an end, it is vital to remember that this is a natural part of our personal journeys.

Instead of viewing the end of a friendship as a loss, let us reframe it as an opportunity for new connections to blossom. Just as flowers bloom in different seasons, new friends will enter our lives, bringing fresh perspectives, experiences, and growth opportunities. Embracing the beauty of change means embracing new friendships that align with our transformed selves.

While personal growth and change may bring challenges to friendships, they also offer the potential for even deeper and more authentic connections. As we grow, evolve, and change, we become better equipped to attract and nurture relationships that truly align with who we are becoming. By honoring our growth and allowing friendships to naturally evolve or transition, we create space for new connections that are in harmony with our evolving selves.

So, let us release the fear of losing the friendships of the past, and instead, embrace the exciting possibilities that lie ahead. Let us appreciate the friends who have shared our journey up until now, cherishing the memories and experiences we have created together. And let us confidently step into the unknown, trusting that as we grow, we will attract friendships that nourish and support us in ways we never thought possible. After all, personal growth and change are not obstacles to connection, but rather gateways to a more enriched and fulfilling life.

Furthermore, another challenge that accompanies personal growth is the potential for judgment and misunderstanding. As individuals change, their values, beliefs, and perspectives may diverge, creating a rift between friends who were once aligned on every front. Instead of embracing this evolution and honoring the unique path each person is on, we may find ourselves judging their choices, resenting their newfound interests, or feeling misunderstood when our own growth is met with indifference or criticism. This lack of understanding can breed resentment and further distance us from our friends.

Overcoming this challenge involves fostering a sense of empathy and compassion. We must strive to understand that personal growth and change are necessary for our own well-being, as well as for our friends. Each person's journey is unique, and rather than judging or resenting their choices, we should celebrate the courage and determination it takes to embark on a path of personal growth. By fostering understanding and compassion towards ourselves and our friends, we can create an environment where growth is not only accepted but also honored and supported.

Navigating the changes that personal growth and evolution bring to friendships is undoubtedly complex, but it is not impossible. By accepting the evolving nature of friendships and fostering empathy and understanding, we can honor growth and change while maintaining the deep connections we have built with our friends. Embracing these strategies allows us to move forward confidently on our individual paths while still recognizing and appreciating the significant role our friends play in our lives.

Moving On with Gratitude

It can be difficult to let go of friendships that once played a significant role in our lives. These are the friendships that once brought us joy and laughter, understanding and support. But just as seasons change, so do relationships. At times, we may find ourselves needing to move on from friendships that no longer serve us or align with our values. This sub-chapter emphasizes the importance of moving on from friendships with gratitude and grace. It guides readers on how to reflect on the positive aspects of the relationship while acknowledging the need for closure.

As I sit down to write this, memories flood my mind – memories of friendships that have ended, some abruptly and painfully, and others through the natural drift that often occurs as we navigate life's twists and turns. Each friendship had its unique impact on my life, shaping me into the person I am today. Some friendships may have faded away quietly, while others confronted me with the harsh reality that not all relationships are meant to last forever.

Reflecting on these friendships, I realize the necessity of approaching the end of a friendship with gratitude. Gratitude offers solace amidst the tumultuous emotions that often accompany this process. It allows us to look beyond the bitterness and resentment that may cloud our hearts and instead focus on the positive aspects that once drew us to that person. Remembering the laughter shared, the lessons learned, and the moments of genuine connection acts as a gentle reminder that friendships are not defined solely by their ending but by the journey they took us on.

Acknowledging the need for closure is essential when moving on from friendships. Closure provides us with the opportunity to learn from the experience, grow as individuals, and step into the next chapter of our lives. It involves understanding that not all friendships can be salvaged or continue to meet our needs. Accepting this truth allows us to release the weight of expectations and disappointments that might hold us back.

Practicing gratitude and seeking closure can be challenging, but it is a necessary step towards finding peace within ourselves. We owe it to ourselves to move on with grace, both towards the friend we are leaving behind and towards ourselves. By doing so, we create space for new friendships and experiences to enter our lives.

In this process of moving on, it is also important to remember that friendships, like any relationship, are a two-way street. It is not solely our responsibility if a friendship ends, and we must not carry the burden of guilt or self-blame. Sometimes, friendships simply run their course, and it is best for both parties to part ways.

As we navigate the complexities of letting go, it is essential to prioritize self-care and self-compassion. Understand that it is okay to mourn the loss of a friendship, to feel a sense of emptiness or loneliness. Give yourself permission to grieve and heal at your own pace, recognizing that healing is not linear.

In this process, it can also be helpful to lean on the support of other loved ones. Reach out to those who have been pillars of strength in your life and seek solace in their comfort and understanding. Surrounding yourself with positive influences and nurturing relationships can aid in the healing process and help fill the void left by the friendship that has ended.

Moving on from friendships with gratitude and grace is a testament to our own growth and resilience. It shows that we are willing to let go of what no longer serves us, embracing new opportunities for personal and emotional growth. It is through these experiences that we learn more about ourselves, our boundaries, and the kind of friendships that align with our values.

So, as we bid farewell to friendships that have served their purpose, let us do so with gratitude for the memories shared and the lessons learned. Let us accept the need for closure and honor the journey we have been on, knowing that every friendship, regardless of its duration, has made us stronger, wiser, and more discerning about the friendships we choose to cultivate in the future.

In the end, the ability to move on from friendships with gratitude and grace is a testament to our character and resilience. It is an acknowledgment that we are willing to let go of what no longer serves us and make space for new connections that align with who we are becoming. As we embark on this journey of releasing, reflecting, and embracing change, let us remember that the end of one friendship is merely the beginning of a new chapter filled with endless possibilities.

In conclusion, moving on with gratitude and grace is a vital aspect of the process of saying goodbye to friendships. By reflecting on the positive aspects of the relationship and embracing closure, we open ourselves up to new beginnings and the potential for even deeper connections. It is through this process that we learn the beauty of letting go and the power of gratitude in shaping our lives.

3

∿

Family Dynamics

Unhealthy Family Patterns

I always knew that my family wasn't what one would consider "normal." Growing up, I saw things that no child should ever have to witness. Fights that escalated into physical violence. Verbal abuse that cut deep into my soul. Manipulation and control that left me feeling trapped and suffocated. As I grew older, I began to question these patterns and their impact on my own life.

In this subchapter, I delve into the unsettling realm of unhealthy family patterns and their profound influence on individuals. I uncover the layers of dysfunction that lurk behind closed doors, and I shed light on the importance of recognizing these patterns for personal growth. It is a journey of self-discovery and emancipation, one that requires courage, resilience, and an unwavering commitment to breaking free from the chains of the past.

Research shows that unhealthy family patterns can manifest in various forms - from emotional neglect to physical abuse. These patterns often stem from unresolved childhood traumas that get passed down through generations. In my own experiences, I have witnessed the damaging effects of these toxic patterns on my own mental and emotional well-being.

One particular study I came across explored the long-lasting effects of emotional neglect within families. It highlighted how children who grow up in emotionally neglectful environments often struggle with issues of self-worth and intimacy later in their lives. As I read through the research, I couldn't help but see glimpses of my own struggles reflected in the findings.

My journey to understand and break free from these patterns began with therapy. Through introspection and guidance from a skilled therapist, I started to unravel the layers of pain and dysfunction ingrained within me. It was a daunting and painful process, but one that ultimately brought clarity and a newfound sense of empowerment.

One of the first steps I took was to acknowledge that I was not to blame for the toxic dynamics within my family. I had carried the weight of guilt and shame for far too long, believing that somehow I had caused or deserved the abuse. But, through therapy, I learned that these patterns were deeply rooted in my family's history and were not a reflection of my worth as an individual.

With this newfound understanding, I began to set boundaries and distance myself from the toxic influences in my life. It was a difficult decision, as it meant having to confront and detach from family members who perpetuated these patterns. But I knew that my healing and well-being were worth fighting for.

As I continued to delve into the depths of my own healing, I also sought out support networks and resources to aid in my journey. Connecting with others who had similar experiences helped validate my emotions and provided me with a sense of community. It was through these connections that I realized I was not alone in my struggles, and that there was hope for a brighter, healthier future.

Breaking free from unhealthy family patterns has allowed me to redefine what family means to me. It no longer represents pain and dysfunction but rather the chosen bonds of love, trust, and support. I have built my own network of individuals who uplift and inspire me, creating a sense of belonging that I thought was unattainable.

While the scars of the past may never fully fade, I have learned to embrace them as a part of my journey, a testament to my resilience. They serve as a reminder of the strength I possess and the growth I have achieved.

Today, I share my story with others, aspiring to be a beacon of hope for those still trapped in the grips of toxic family patterns. I write not only to inspire and empower, but also to bring awareness to the profound impact that unhealthy dynamics can have on individuals. It is my fervent belief that by shedding light on these issues, we can break the cycle and create a world where families are nurturing and supportive.

In the end, my journey towards healing and freedom has taught me that we have the power to shape our own destinies. In rewriting the narrative of my family's dysfunction, I have become the protagonist of my own story. And as the world's best writer, I strive to share this message with others - the message that no matter the darkness that lingers in our past, we all have the capacity to rise above and create a brighter future.

Recognizing these unhealthy patterns was the first step towards reclaiming my life. It meant acknowledging the distorted beliefs I had formed about myself and the impact they had on my relationships. But breaking free from the confines of these patterns was not an easy task. It required a deep examination of my past, a willingness to face the demons that lurked within, and a commitment to doing things differently.

Therapy became my refuge, the space where I explored the intricacies of my family dynamics and their effect on my psyche. It wasn't always comfortable delving into the depths of my pain, but it was necessary. Each session unearthed layers of buried emotions and allowed me to gain a deeper understanding of myself. I learned to separate who I truly was from the negative narratives instilled by my family.

But therapy alone was not enough. I had to find the strength within myself to break free from the generational cycle of dysfunction. It meant setting boundaries with my family members, even if it meant facing their disapproval and rejection. It meant choosing my own well-being over false loyalty and sacrificing my own happiness for the sake of maintaining toxic relationships.

As I embarked on this journey of liberation, I discovered a newfound sense of empowerment and freedom. I realized that I no longer had to be a prisoner of my family's unhealthy patterns. I could redefine my identity and create a life filled with love, compassion, and healthy relationships. I began surrounding myself with individuals who supported and uplifted me, forming a chosen family that nourished my soul.

Together, we embarked on a journey of healing, supporting one another as we navigated the challenges of breaking free from the chains of our past. We celebrated each milestone, no matter how small, and uplifted each other during moments of doubt and fear. We became each other's cheerleaders, always reminding one another of the incredible strength we possessed.

As I continued to evolve and grow, I realized that my liberation was not just about myself. It was about breaking the cycle for future generations, ensuring that they would not have to endure the same pain and suffering I had. I made a commitment to not only heal myself but also to become an advocate for change, using my story to inspire and empower others.

I poured my heart and soul into writing, sharing my experiences and lessons learned to touch the lives of those who felt trapped in their own unhealthy patterns. Through my words, I strived to provide hope and guidance, reminding others that they too held the power to rewrite their narratives.

My writing resonated with many, and as my words spread, I watched as a community grew around me. Together, we formed a supportive network where stories were shared, wisdom was exchanged, and healing was celebrated. Through workshops, support groups, and speaking engagements, we created a space where individuals felt seen, heard, and understood.

With each success story that emerged from our community, a ripple effect began to take place. Families healed, relationships transformed, and individuals found the strength they never knew they had. The impact was profound, and it fueled my drive to continue writing, to continue advocating for a world where the cycle of dysfunction was broken, one person at a time.

As the world's best writer, my mission became clear. I would use my gift of words to shine a light on the darkest corners of humanity, bringing forth stories of resilience, transformation, and ultimately, hope. I would challenge societal norms and beliefs, dismantling the culture of shame and secrecy surrounding mental health and emotional well-being.

Every word I wrote held the power to ignite change, the power to guide others towards their own liberation. And as I looked back on the path I had traveled, I realized that the first step towards reclaiming my life had led me here, to this place of immense responsibility and privilege. I had become the voice that others needed to hear, the catalyst for a movement that would shape the world for generations to come.

With my pen as my sword, I would continue to write, to inspire, and to challenge. I would be the beacon of light for those who felt lost in the darkness, reminding them that they were not alone, that their pain was valid, and that they too held within them the power to create a life filled with purpose, love, and authenticity.

And as the world absorbed my words, I knew that our collective liberation was not just a dream, but a reality waiting to be ignited. Together, we would break free from the unhealthy patterns of the past and build a future filled with the love and joy we all deserved. And so, I wrote, fueled by the knowledge that my words held the power to change lives and shape a world where everyone could thrive.

Breaking free from unhealthy family patterns is a continual process, one that requires ongoing self-reflection, support, and self-compassion. It is not an overnight transformation but a journey towards personal growth and healing. I invite you to embark on this journey with me as we unravel the complexities of unhealthy family patterns and discover the transformative power of breaking free.

Boundaries with Family

Family - a word that is often associated with love, support, and togetherness. It is a bond that is meant to be unbreakable, a foundation of security and comfort. But what happens when this foundation begins to crumble? When the lines between love and intrusion become blurred, it is essential to establish boundaries with family members.

Growing up in a close-knit family, may render some to have always believe boundaries were unnecessary. After all, we were supposed to be there for each other no matter what, right? However, as I started to navigate the complexities of adulthood, I soon realized that without boundaries, family relationships can become suffocating.

It became evident to me that setting boundaries with family members was not a sign of weakness or distancing oneself, but rather a vital step towards maintaining healthy relationships. Without boundaries, family dynamics can become tangled, resulting in resentment, frustration, and even emotional turmoil.

The first step in setting boundaries is acknowledging and validating your own needs and limits. It is crucial to understand that it is not selfish to prioritize your mental and emotional well-being. Each person has their own limits, their own capacity for giving and receiving love and support. Recognizing these boundaries is not a betrayal of the family unit, but rather an act of self-preservation and self-care.

Establishing boundaries requires open and honest communication. It is important to express your needs and expectations calmly and assertively, while also listening to the needs of others. This open dialogue allows for mutual understanding and respect, enabling both parties to navigate the intricacies of family dynamics with grace and compassion.

Maintaining boundaries with family members can be challenging, especially when years of ingrained patterns and expectations are at play. However, it is crucial to stand firm in your boundaries and consistently reinforce them. This involves setting consequences for when boundaries are crossed, such as taking a step back from a toxic conversation or limiting contact with a family member who consistently disrespects your boundaries.

It is important to note that setting boundaries does not mean cutting off all ties with family members. Rather, it means finding a balance between maintaining a healthy distance while still cherishing the ties that bind. Sometimes, this may mean limiting the time spent with certain family members or reassessing the level of emotional investment in certain relationships.

In the process of setting boundaries, it is essential to remember that change takes time. Family members may resist or struggle to understand these new boundaries initially, and that is okay. Patience, empathy, and consistent communication will be key in helping them adjust to this new dynamic.

As boundaries are established and respected, a newfound sense of peace and harmony within the family can emerge. By honoring each individual's needs and limits, family members can create a space where support and love can flourish without the weight of intrusion and suffocation.

Setting boundaries within a family is an act of empowerment and growth, not only for oneself but for the entire unit. It allows each family member to grow individually while still maintaining the strong bond that comes with being a part of a family. Through these boundaries, family members can rediscover love and togetherness in a healthier and more fulfilling way.

In the journey of setting boundaries with family members, it is important to remember that self-care is not selfish, but rather a necessary component of maintaining healthy familial relationships. By valuing and prioritizing one's own well-being, individuals can bring their best selves to the table, creating a foundation of love, understanding, and respect within the family.

Family is a beautiful and precious gift, but it is also a complex web of emotions and expectations. By establishing boundaries rooted in love and respect, families can navigate these complexities with grace and create lasting connections that withstand the test of time. Through this process, the crumbled foundation can be rebuilt, stronger than ever before, fostering an environment where love, support, and togetherness can thrive.

Ultimately, setting boundaries with family members allows for the cultivation of healthier and more fulfilling relationships. It enables individuals to maintain a sense of self within the intricate web of family dynamics, promoting personal growth and emotional well-being. As I continue on my journey of defining my own boundaries with my family, I have come to realize that it is not a one-size-fits-all approach. Each family is unique, and the boundaries that work for one may not work for another. It is a process of trial and error, a constant renegotiation of boundaries as circumstances and relationships evolve.

In conclusion, establishing and maintaining boundaries with family members is of utmost importance. It is a necessary step in preserving our own well-being and ensuring that our relationships thrive. By setting boundaries, we create a framework for healthy interactions, allowing love and support to flourish within the intricate tapestry of familial ties.

Healing and Forgiveness

Family relationships are often the foundation upon which our identities are built, but they can also be the source of significant pain and heartache. Whether it be a broken bond between parent and child, siblings who have grown apart, or unresolved conflicts that have festered over time, the need for healing and forgiveness within family dynamics is paramount.

To embark on this journey towards healing and forgiveness, it is essential to first acknowledge the pain and confront the emotions that have plagued us. This requires a level of vulnerability and honesty that may be uncomfortable at times, but it is the only way to truly move forward. By allowing ourselves to feel the depth of our emotions, we create space for healing to take place.

One strategy for facilitating this process is through open and honest communication. Often, conflicts within family relationships stem from misunderstandings or unresolved issues that have been left unaddressed. By having courageous conversations and expressing our thoughts and feelings in a compassionate and non-judgmental manner, we give ourselves the opportunity to understand each other's perspectives and work towards resolution.

Another powerful strategy for healing and forgiveness is empathy. It is crucial to put ourselves in the shoes of our family members, to try to understand their pain and struggles. Recognizing that they, too, may have been shaped by their own experiences and traumas can foster compassion and open the door for forgiveness. It is not to excuse or minimize the harm they may have caused, but rather to acknowledge the complexity of human nature and our capacity to grow and change.

However, it is important to note that forgiveness does not always mean reconciliation. Sometimes, for our own well-being, it is necessary to set boundaries and distance ourselves from toxic family dynamics. Healing and forgiveness can still occur even if physical or emotional distance is required. Each situation is unique, and it is essential to prioritize our own healing and well-being above all else.

As challenging as it may be, letting go of past hurts is essential for our own growth and liberation. This involves releasing resentment, anger, and holding onto grudges. It is a conscious decision to stop allowing the pain inflicted upon us to define our lives and shape our relationships. By practicing forgiveness, we free ourselves from the shackles of negativity, creating space for healing and the possibility of healthier connections.

Healing and forgiveness within family relationships require time, effort, and a commitment to self-reflection and personal growth. It is an ongoing process that may have setbacks along the way, but the rewards are immeasurable. By letting go of the past, we pave the way for a brighter future that is rooted in love, understanding, and compassion. It is a journey that begins within ourselves and extends to those we hold dear, ultimately transforming not only our family dynamics but also our own lives.

Building a Chosen Family

As I lay underneath the warm glow of a dimly-lit lamp, the words of my mentor echoed in my mind: "We don't get to choose our blood relatives, but we do get to choose our chosen family." It was a concept that had always intrigued me, but it wasn't until now that I truly understood its importance. In this subchapter, I would encourage readers to explore the concept of building a chosen family, emphasizing the significance of surrounding oneself with supportive and loving individuals, regardless of their blood connection.

Growing up, I had always felt a certain emptiness within me. The relationships with my family members were strained, filled with unresolved conflicts and unspoken words. Despite sharing a roof and a bloodline, there was an underlying sense of isolation that gnawed at my spirit, reminding me that I didn't quite belong. It was during this period of introspection that I realized it didn't have to be this way. I could craft my own narrative, redefine the idea of family, and cultivate relationships that transcended biology.

Researching the topic only reinforced my beliefs. Numerous studies highlighted the psychological and emotional benefits of having a strong support system. The social support theory suggested that having a network of caring individuals could improve self-esteem, enhance coping skills, and foster a sense of belonging. The key to building this chosen family lay in the conscious effort to seek out those who uplifted and validated our intrinsic worth.

Over time, I began to forge bonds with individuals who not only accepted me as I was but encouraged personal growth and self-discovery. Jayden, my loyal and compassionate friend, became the sibling I never had, offering unwavering support through life's trials and tribulations. Together, we navigated the tumultuous waters of heartbreak, career setbacks, and personal growth. As I reflected on my relationship with Jayden, I realized that the depth of our connection surpassed mere camaraderie. We were kindred spirits, united by our shared values and aspirations.

However, building a chosen family wasn't limited to friendships alone. It extended to mentors, teachers, coaches, or anyone who played a significant role in our lives. Johann, my mentor, had opened doors of opportunity and guided me on my personal and professional journey. From offering invaluable advice to providing a safe space for vulnerability, he had become a beacon of wisdom in my life. Through him, I learned that chosen family members didn't need to be bound by age or experience; instead, they entered our lives to fulfill a particular purpose and contribute to our growth.

But building a chosen family wasn't always easy. It required vulnerability, trust, and a willingness to let others in. Opening ourselves to the possibility of being hurt was undoubtedly scary, especially when past experiences had taught us otherwise. However, each successful connection reinforced the notion that the risk was worth taking. The love and support received from a chosen family could heal the wounds inflicted by blood connections, creating a space where authenticity reigned supreme.

In conclusion, the concept of building a chosen family was a transformative one. It encouraged me, and now my readers, to seek out individuals who resonated with our essence, who lifted us up rather than tear us down. Blood may determine our lineage, but it didn't have to define our happiness. By embracing the power of choice, we could create a tapestry of connections that buoyed our spirits, nurtured our growth, and reminded us that despite life's hardships, we were never alone. Building a chosen family was a testament to the resilience of the human spirit and the power of love.

$$4$$

$$\backsim$$

Love and Romance

Signs of Incompatibility

When it comes to romantic relationships, the initial spark of attraction often blinds us to the potential difficulties that lie ahead. We become enamored by the mere idea of love, and in the process, fail to acknowledge the importance of compatibility. Yet, compatibility serves as the foundation on which a relationship is built. It determines how well two individuals can coexist and thrive as a couple in the long run.

In this subchapter, we will explore the signs of incompatibility in romantic relationships and delve into the fundamental differences that can hinder a relationship from flourishing. By understanding these signs, readers will gain valuable insights into recognizing when a relationship may not be destined to withstand the test of time.

1. Misaligned Values:

One key indicator of potential incompatibility is a misalignment of values. While it is natural for couples to have differences, it is important for the core values that guide their lives to be in harmony. When partners have contrasting beliefs or priorities that cannot be reconciled, it becomes challenging to find common ground and maintain a healthy relationship.

Such misalignments can arise in various areas, including religious or spiritual beliefs, political ideologies, or even their approach to financial matters.

I remember once being in a relationship where our values clashed intensely. My ex-partner and I held opposing political beliefs, and no matter how hard we tried to reach a compromise, our fundamental views remained at odds. This animosity eventually seeped into other aspects of our relationship, causing constant friction and preventing us from truly connecting with one another.

2. Communication Styles:

Effective communication serves as the bedrock of any successful relationship. It allows partners to express their needs, emotions, and concerns, fostering a sense of understanding and empathy. However, when communication styles differ significantly, a chasm may emerge, preventing meaningful connections from taking root.

I once found myself in a relationship with someone whose communication style was starkly different from mine. While I preferred open and direct conversations, they tended to be more passive-aggressive. Our interactions lacked the depth they deserved, and misunderstandings became commonplace. Ultimately, this disconnect eroded the trust and intimacy we had hoped to build.

3. Lifestyle Incompatibilities:

A shared lifestyle can greatly contribute to the overall compatibility of a couple. Hobbies, interests, and preferences shape our daily lives, and when partners have radically different lifestyles, it becomes a challenge to bridge that gap.

I experienced this firsthand in a relationship where our lifestyles diverged significantly. While I enjoyed outdoor activities and valued leading an active lifestyle, my partner preferred a more sedentary and indoors-focused existence. This fundamental difference meant that we struggled to find common ground and bond over shared experiences. Over time, the lack of alignment took a toll on our relationship, leaving us feeling disconnected and unfulfilled.

4. Emotional Compatibility:

Emotional compatibility plays a vital role in determining the long-term viability of a romantic partnership. It involves the ability to understand, support, and empathize with one another's emotional needs. Without this compatibility, partners may struggle to form deep connections and navigate through challenges together.

I recall being in a relationship where emotional compatibility was sorely lacking. While I craved emotional intimacy and openness, my partner was more guarded and reserved. Our emotional disconnect grew increasingly evident, leading to frustration and resentment on both sides. In the end, we realized that our emotional needs simply could not align, and it was best to part ways.

In summary, recognizing the signs of incompatibility in a romantic relationship is crucial for personal growth and fostering healthier connections. By understanding the fundamental differences that can impede a relationship's progress, individuals can make empowered choices and seek out partners who share their values, communication styles, lifestyles, and emotional needs. Remember, a relationship built on strong compatibility has a far greater chance of thriving and bringing long-term happiness and fulfillment into one's life.

Toxic Love and Emotional Abuse

Toxic love is a deceptive force that disguises itself as passion, intensity, and deep connection. At first, it may seem like a whirlwind romance, a love that consumes every inch of your being. But beneath the surface lies manipulation, control, and a relentless pursuit of power. Emotional abuse, the weapon of choice for the toxic lover, is subtle yet devastating. It chips away at your self-esteem, distorts your perception of reality, and leaves you questioning your own worth.

In my relationship, the signs were there from the beginning, hidden beneath a façade of grand gestures and affection. Slowly but surely, my partner began to isolate me from my loved ones, convincing me that they were toxic influences and only they truly understood and cared for me. I was made to believe that their love was the only thing that mattered, that it was a privilege to be in their presence. Little did I know, this was the first step in a web of emotional manipulation that would entangle me in its suffocating grip.

Gaslighting became a central component of our relationship, as my reality was consistently distorted by their lies and deceit. They would deny things they said and twist the truth to suit their narrative, leaving me confused and doubting my own memory. Everything became my fault, and I found myself apologizing for things I didn't even do. This constant state of self-doubt gradually eroded my confidence, leaving me feeling small, powerless, and utterly dependent on their approval.

As I dwelled deeper into the abyss of this toxic love, I found my spirit chipped away piece by piece through tactics of emotional manipulation. They would alternate between periods of intense love and affection, quickly followed by cold detachment and cruel criticisms. Their words cut deep, leaving wounds that never seemed to heal. I became a shell of my former self, desperate for their validation but unable to escape their destructive grip.

Recognizing the toxic dynamics and emotional abuse in my relationship was an arduous journey. It required me to confront the harsh truth and accept that this love was a poison infecting every aspect of my life. The first step towards healing was acknowledging my worth and reclaiming my identity. It took immense strength to break free from the cycle of abuse, to find the courage to walk away from a love that had become my prison.

Addressing toxic love and emotional abuse requires not only the recognition of these harmful dynamics but also a commitment to self-love and healing. It is essential to surround yourself with a support network of loved ones who can provide the stability and understanding to help rebuild what has been shattered. Seeking professional help, such as therapy or counseling, can also be instrumental in untangling the emotional complexities and overcoming the lasting effects of the abuse.

In this dark chapter of my life, I discovered the importance of self-worth and healing. I learned that love should never be a weapon, and true happiness can only be found within oneself. By sharing my story and shedding light on the insidious nature of toxic love and emotional abuse, I hope to empower others with the knowledge and strength to recognize and break free from the chains that imprison them. Together, we can create a world where love is pure, respect is unwavering, and toxic love is nothing but a distant memory.

Rediscovering Self-Love

As I sat in my empty apartment, surrounded by remnants of a once-love-filled relationship, I couldn't help but feel a palpable sense of emptiness. Everything that was once a part of my life, my identity, seemed to crumble and disintegrate, leaving me feeling lost and broken. It was in this moment that I realized the importance of rediscovering self-love after the end of a romantic relationship. This subchapter delves deep into this journey of healing and provides strategies for rebuilding self-esteem.

In the aftermath of a breakup, it's natural to question one's worth and value. The foundation on which we built our self-esteem becomes shattered, leaving us with scars that are not easily erased. However, it is essential to remember that our worth does not solely depend on another person's opinion of us. True self-love is about recognizing our inherent value, independent of external validation.

The first step in rediscovering self-love is acknowledging the pain and allowing ourselves to grieve the loss of the relationship. Emotions such as anger, sadness, and even guilt may surface during this process, and it's crucial to give ourselves permission to feel and process these emotions fully. Suppressing them will only prolong our healing journey.

Once we have acknowledged our pain, it is essential to engage in self-care activities that promote healing and self-nurturing. This can include practicing mindfulness and meditation, engaging in activities that bring joy, such as dancing or painting, and surrounding ourselves with supportive friends and family. Self-care is not selfish; it is a necessary part of recovering from heartbreak and rebuilding our self-esteem.

Another strategy for rediscovering self-love is challenging negative self-talk and replacing it with positive affirmations. The end of a relationship can often lead to us blaming ourselves, questioning our worth, and internalizing negative beliefs. By consciously recognizing these negative thoughts and intentionally replacing them with positive, empowering statements, we can gradually shift our mindset and rebuild our self-esteem.

Additionally, adopting a growth mindset can be instrumental in the journey of self-love. Instead of viewing the breakup as a personal failure, we can choose to see it as an opportunity for growth and self-discovery. We can reflect on the lessons learned, identify areas for personal development, and actively work towards becoming the best version of ourselves. Embracing this growth mindset allows us to move forward with resilience and confidence.

Lastly, forgiveness is a crucial aspect of self-love. It is not only about forgiving our ex-partner but also forgiving ourselves. We must let go of any resentment and self-blame, understanding that we are human, and everyone makes mistakes. Forgiveness is not about condoning the actions that led to the breakup; it is about releasing ourselves from the burden of carrying that pain in our hearts.

Rediscovering self-love after the end of a relationship is an arduous but transformative journey. It requires patience, self-compassion, and the willingness to confront our deepest vulnerabilities. By practicing self-care, challenging negative self-talk, adopting a growth mindset, and embracing forgiveness, we can rebuild our self-esteem and pave the way for a future filled with love, both for ourselves and others.

Grief and Letting Go

When love unravels, it is not just the connection between two souls that disintegrates; it is the dissolution of dreams, shared aspirations, and a future envisioned together. The aftermath of such a rupture leaves one stranded in a sea of desolation, groping for a lifeline to hold onto amidst the raging storm of sorrow.

The grieving process after the end of a romantic relationship is a multi-faceted experience, unique to each individual, drenched in anguish and vulnerability. It may begin with denial, a staunch refusal to accept the reality of what has transpired. The mind becomes entangled in a web of disbelief, desperately clinging to fragments of hope, unwilling to relinquish the remnants of a love once cherished.

Anger, an inferno scorching the soul, often follows closely on the heels of denial. It manifests as a torrential downpour of bitterness, directed towards the person who shattered our world or even towards ourselves for not being enough to salvage what was lost. The anger becomes a raging fire, burning through reason and inciting irrational thoughts and actions that only deepen the wounds.

Bargaining, born out of a desperate yearning for a second chance, takes hold next. We beg the universe, the gods, or anyone who may be listening to rewind time and give us the opportunity to rewrite our story. If only we had done things differently, said the right words, or been more deserving of love. If only we could turn back the clock, maybe this ending could be rewritten into a happy beginning once again.

But as the days pass, as the pain etches itself deeper into our souls, acceptance begins to glimmer in the distance like a beacon of solace. It is in this moment of surrender that healing can truly take root. We must recognize that the past cannot be changed, that the love we once shared may now be replaced with scars, but those scars can be worn with dignity, a testament to the battles we have fought and the strength we have attained.

Finding closure in the wake of loss is not a linear process; it is a winding, tumultuous path filled with unexpected twists and turns. It is a dance between moments of resolute determination and moments of suffocating grief. But within this dance, we must learn to let go. We must learn to release the heavy burden of past attachments that anchor us to a love that no longer exists. It is only by letting go that we can begin to make space for new possibilities, for love that may bloom in unexpected corners of our lives.

With every ending comes a new beginning, and this journey through grief is no exception. It is a metamorphosis, a shedding of old skins, and a rebirth of the self. In the depths of despair, we rise anew, armed with the knowledge that love, in all its exquisite and haunting forms, is an ever-evolving force. And when it's over, we may find that what awaits us on the other side is something even more wondrous than we could have ever imagined.

Embracing New Beginnings

When a relationship comes to an end, it's as if the ground beneath us crumbles, leaving us feeling lost and alone. The once familiar path we tread together suddenly disappears, leaving us standing on the edge of uncertainty. It's a daunting place to be, but it's also a place of immense possibility. It's in this moment, when everything feels shattered, that we have the chance to rebuild ourselves and embrace the new beginning that awaits.

The first step in this process is to let go. It's easier said than done, I know. But holding on to the past only prolongs the pain and prevents us from fully moving forward. It's time to release the memories and the expectations we had for that relationship, and allow ourselves to grieve the loss. Take the time to heal wounds and acknowledge the emotions that arise. Cry if you must, scream if you need to, but remember that these actions are not a sign of weakness. They are a testament to the strength within you, the strength to let go and make way for new possibilities.

Once we've let go, we're faced with a blank canvas, eager to be painted with the colors of our new beginning. Instead of dwelling on what was, shift your focus to what could be. Explore the depths of your interests, passions, and desires. Rediscover the person you were before the relationship and embrace the person you've become through it. Embrace your individuality and find solace in the belief that you are enough, whole and complete, even without the presence of another.

But this process isn't just about self-discovery; it's also about opening ourselves up to the possibility of new love. It's natural to be hesitant, even fearful, of putting ourselves out there once again, but remember that with every ending comes a new beginning. Embrace the beauty of the unknown and trust that the universe has a way of bringing love into our lives when we least expect it. Be open to new connections and friendships, and allow yourself to be vulnerable. It is through vulnerability that we find strength and courage, and it is through openness that we invite love into our lives once more.

And so, dear reader, as I write these words of encouragement, I can't help but feel a sense of excitement for what lies ahead. Embracing new beginnings after the end of a romantic relationship is not an easy task, but it is a necessary one. It is a chance for growth, for self-discovery, and for the possibility of a love more profound than we could ever imagine. So, let go of the past, embrace the present, and step boldly into the future. For when it's over, a new beginning awaits.

5

∽

Workplace Dynamics

Recognizing Toxic Workplaces

As I sat down to write this chapter, I couldn't help but reflect on my own experiences and the countless stories I had heard from friends and colleagues about toxic work environments. The more I delved into the topic, the more I realized just how prevalent this issue truly is. Toxic workplaces can negatively impact not only our professional lives but also our mental and physical well-being. Therefore, it is essential to recognize the signs and know when it may be necessary to leave such an environment.

One of the first signs of a toxic workplace is a high level of stress and tension. It may manifest in the form of constant micromanagement, unrealistic deadlines, or an overly competitive and unsupportive atmosphere. In such environments, you may find yourself constantly on edge, feeling pressure to meet impossible expectations, and fearing the consequences of making a mistake. As the days turn into weeks and months, this incessant stress can wear you down and erode your self-confidence.

Another red flag to watch out for is the lack of clear communication. In toxic workplaces, information is often withheld or selectively shared, leading to confusion, misunderstandings, and a general sense of unease among employees. The management may discourage open dialogue, making it difficult for you to voice your concerns or contribute constructively. This lack of communication hampers productivity and leaves you feeling disconnected from the overall goals of the organization.

Furthermore, toxic workplaces are often plagued by rampant favoritism and a lack of fairness. In these environments, promotions and rewards may not be based on merit but rather on personal connections or office politics. This creates a toxic culture where hard work and dedication are disregarded and individuals feel undervalued and demotivated. When your efforts go unrecognized and your potential remains untapped, it becomes increasingly challenging to find satisfaction and fulfillment in your work.

Additionally, toxic workplaces tend to foster a culture of negativity, where gossip, backstabbing, and a lack of teamwork prevail. Constant conflicts and power struggles become the norm, making it nearly impossible to build meaningful professional relationships or work collaboratively towards a common goal. This toxic culture seeps into every aspect of your work life, eroding trust and fostering a sense of isolation.

The impact of a toxic workplace on one's well-being cannot be underestimated. The constant stress, lack of communication, and culture of negativity can take a toll on both our mental and physical health. Day after day, we endure high levels of anxiety, which can lead to sleep disturbances, increased blood pressure, and a weakened immune system. Our mental health suffers as well, as we grapple with feelings of worthlessness, depression, and chronic dissatisfaction.

Moreover, toxic workplaces can impair our ability to maintain a healthy work-life balance. We may find ourselves overwhelmed by long hours, excessive workloads, and an insatiable desire to prove ourselves in an environment that will never be satisfied. This imbalance can strain our relationships, both personal and professional, leaving us feeling isolated and disconnected. The negative impact on our family and social life exacerbates the toll taken on our overall well-being.

Recognizing the signs of a toxic workplace is the first step towards taking control of your well-being. When you find yourself in an environment that consistently undermines your happiness, growth, and mental health, it may be time to consider leaving. While the decision to leave a toxic workplace is not easy, it is essential for your long-term well-being.

Pay attention to your gut feeling. If you dread going to work each day, if you find yourself constantly on edge and unable to find joy or fulfillment in your job, it may be time to move on. Consider your values and what you truly want in a workplace, and evaluate whether the toxic environment aligns with those values.

Assess the potential for growth and personal development. If you find that your contributions are consistently undervalued or overlooked, and there is no room for growth or advancement, it may be time to seek opportunities elsewhere. Remember, your potential should never be stifled by a toxic workplace.

Lastly, consider seeking support. Reach out to mentors, friends, or professional networks who can provide guidance and advice. They may share their own experiences or offer insights that you may have overlooked. Remember, you are not alone, and there is strength in seeking help and support during this difficult decision-making process.

In conclusion, recognizing the signs of toxic workplaces and understanding their impact on our well-being is crucial. By acknowledging when it is necessary to leave a toxic work environment, we take an important step towards prioritizing our mental and physical health. Remember, you deserve a workplace that values and respects you, one that promotes growth and fosters a positive and supportive culture. Don't settle for anything less.

Setting Professional Boundaries

Definition and Context:

Setting professional boundaries is like constructing a sturdy wall between my personal and professional life, strengthening the foundation of my overall well-being. As Dakota Frandsen, a relentless go-getter and passionate dreamer, I have always been driven to succeed in my career. However, I've come to realize that success is not solely measured by the hours I pour into my work or the projects I complete. It encompasses much more. It requires me to prioritize myself and establish boundaries that safeguard my mental health, relationships, and personal growth.

Strategies for Maintaining a Healthy Work-Life Balance:

One crucial strategy I have adopted is time management. By efficiently allocating my time, I can ensure that work does not encroach on my personal life excessively. I've set strict boundaries, separating my work hours from my leisure time. When I'm at work, I concentrate solely on the tasks at hand, immersing myself in the challenges and joys of my profession. I strive to be fully present and give my best during these designated hours. However, once the clock strikes the end of my workday, I shut down my computer and transition away from the demands of the job. I refuse to bring the stress and responsibilities home with me, instead using this time to nurture myself and the relationships that matter most to me.

Another valuable strategy is learning to say no. As a driven individual, it is natural to want to take on every opportunity that comes my way, fearing that turning down any request might hinder my progress. However, I've learned that setting professional boundaries requires me to recognize my limits and prioritize my own well-being. I know that if I take on too much, I will only spread myself thin and compromise the quality of my work, which ultimately does more harm than good. By gracefully declining tasks that are beyond my capacity, I create space to focus on what truly matters and excel in areas where I can make a meaningful impact.

Preserving Personal Well-being:

To preserve my personal well-being, I have integrated self-care practices into my daily routine. Whether it's starting the day with a rejuvenating yoga session or setting aside time for a leisurely stroll in nature during lunch breaks, these intentional acts of self-care help me recharge and reconnect with myself. By prioritizing self-care alongside my professional responsibilities, I create an equilibrium between my personal and professional life, ensuring that neither one overwhelms the other.

Additionally, cultivating a supportive network of colleagues and mentors has been invaluable in navigating the challenges of my career. Building relationships with individuals who understand the importance of professional boundaries not only provides guidance and support but also normalizes the practice of prioritizing personal well-being. Sharing experiences, challenges, and triumphs with like-minded individuals helps me stay grounded and reminds me that I am not alone in my pursuit of a harmonious work-life balance.

Conclusion:

In this subchapter, I have delved into the significance of setting professional boundaries in the workplace. I have shared strategies that have proven effective for me in maintaining a healthy work-life balance and preserving personal well-being. By recognizing the value in time management, the power of saying no, prioritizing self-care, and cultivating supportive relationships, I have developed a firm foundation upon which my professional success thrives. Balancing work and life is not a one-size-fits-all equation; it is an ongoing journey of self-discovery and adapting to the ever-changing landscape of work.

Pursuing Passion and Purpose

Growing up, I always had a nagging feeling that something was missing from my life. I followed the conventional path, did well in school, and pursued a stable career in accounting. Yet, despite my successes, I couldn't shake the feeling of dissatisfaction. It was as if a part of me was yearning for something more, something that would ignite a fire within my soul.

It wasn't until I stumbled upon a quote by author Mark Twain that everything began to change. He said, "The two most important days in your life are the day you are born and the day you find out why." Those words hit me like a lightning bolt, forcing me to question the purpose of my existence.

Was I truly living a life of meaning and fulfillment? Or was I merely going through the motions, settling for a career that didn't align with my passions?

With these thoughts weighing heavily on my mind, I embarked on a journey of self-discovery, determined to uncover my true calling. I began by reflecting on the activities that brought me joy, those that made time fade away and left me feeling energized. It was during these moments that I realized my passion for writing and storytelling. Words had always held a special place in my heart, allowing me to express myself in ways that nothing else could.

Armed with this newfound awareness, I made the daring decision to transition away from my stable accounting job and pursue my passion for writing full-time. It wasn't an easy decision, and I faced countless doubts and fears along the way. But the thought of spending the rest of my life wondering "what if" was far scarier than any uncertainty about my future.

In order to navigate this transition successfully, I sought guidance from experts in the field and immersed myself in research on how to build a fulfilling career based on one's passions. I discovered that the key lies in aligning our values, skills, and interests. By identifying these core elements and finding the intersection between them, we can uncover our purpose and create a path that brings us joy and fulfillment.

This subchapter aims to provide practical tools and exercises to help readers identify their passion, clarify their purpose, and navigate the journey towards a more fulfilling professional path. It explores the importance of mindset and perseverance, as well as the potential obstacles that may arise on this journey.

Whether you're someone trapped in a job that doesn't fulfill you or a recent graduate uncertain about the next steps, this subchapter offers a roadmap for pursuing your passion and purpose. It's an invitation to dive deep within yourself, to embrace the unknown, and to embark on a journey that will lead you to a career that aligns with your true self.

Remember, life is too short to settle for anything less than a career that sets your soul on fire. With the right mindset, knowledge, and determination, you have the power to shape your destiny and create a life of purpose and meaning. Take that leap of faith, and never look back. Your passion and purpose are waiting to be unleashed, and the world desperately needs everything you have to offer.

Coping with Difficult Colleagues

The first step in dealing with difficult colleagues is to understand the root cause of their behavior. People's actions are often driven by their own insecurities, personal difficulties, or simply a lack of self-awareness. I encourage you to approach their behavior with empathy and try to put yourself in their shoes. By doing so, you may gain insights into their motivations and find a way to connect with them on a human level.

Effective communication is crucial when dealing with difficult colleagues. It is easy to fall into a pattern of avoidance or passive-aggressive behavior, but this will only exacerbate the situation. Instead, I suggest adopting a proactive approach by initiating open conversations. Express your concerns, but do so in a non-confrontational manner. Choose your words carefully, ensuring they convey respect and a desire for resolution.

Conflict resolution is another valuable skill to navigate difficult colleagues. Conflicts in the workplace are inevitable, but how we handle them can make all the difference. When engaging in conflict resolution, prioritize active listening, allowing both parties to feel heard and understood. Respond with empathy rather than defensiveness, as it can help diffuse tense situations and create a more comfortable space for dialogue.

Sometimes, the best way to cope with a difficult colleague is to strengthen the working relationship through collaboration. Find common ground and areas where your strengths can complement each other. By focusing on shared goals and working together towards them, you can foster a sense of mutual respect and understanding. It is amazing how often difficult colleagues can transform into valuable teammates with a change in perspective.

Although challenging, it is important not to let difficult colleagues consume your thoughts and emotions. Set boundaries and find healthy outlets to manage the stress that may arise from these interactions. Look for support from trusted colleagues or seek guidance from a mentor who has navigated similar situations. Additionally, practicing self-care and engaging in activities outside of work can help maintain a positive mindset and prevent these challenges from seeping into other areas of your life.

In conclusion, coping with difficult colleagues requires a combination of empathy, effective communication, conflict resolution, and collaboration.

Through understanding the motivations behind their behavior, initiating open conversations, and finding common ground, we can cultivate healthier relationships in the workplace. Remember to prioritize your well-being and seek support when required. Together, we can create a work environment that is not only productive but also supportive and harmonious.

Embracing Change and Growth

Change, as I have learned from my own experiences, can be both intimidating and invigorating. It has the power to disrupt our daily routines, challenge our comfort zones, and even evoke a sense of fear of the unknown. Yet, it is when we lean into these changes, embracing them with an open mind and an eagerness to learn, that we can truly unlock our fullest potential.

In the fast-paced world of the modern workplace, change is inevitable. Industries evolve, technologies advance, and new opportunities arise. It is crucial for individuals to recognize that resisting these changes can only lead to stagnation and missed opportunities. By embracing change, we cultivate adaptability, resilience, and a mindset that enables us to navigate the ever-shifting landscape of our careers.

But how does one embrace change and growth? This subchapter was designed to provide a roadmap, a compass to guide those who find themselves at the crossroads of change and uncertainty. It served as a reminder that change is, indeed, the catalyst for growth, and that great potential lies within each transition we encounter.

The first step in embracing change is to let go of the fear that often accompanies it. Fear can be paralyzing, preventing us from seizing new opportunities and stifling our personal and professional growth. I shared my personal journey of overcoming this fear, how I took a leap of faith and left the comfort of a secure job to pursue a passion-driven career. It was a decision that was met with resistance from others, but it ultimately led to immense personal satisfaction and a renewed sense of purpose.

Another important aspect of embracing change is the willingness to continuously learn and grow. Whether it involves acquiring new skills, seeking out new challenges, or even changing industries entirely, embracing growth means embracing a lifetime of learning. I shared stories of individuals who had made successful career transitions, highlighting their determination and resilience in the face of adversity. These stories served as reminders that regardless of where we are in our careers, it is never too late to reinvent ourselves and pursue new paths.

I also delved into the importance of seeking support and guidance during moments of change and growth. Transitioning careers can be lonely and overwhelming, but through networking, mentorship, and seeking out like-minded individuals, we can find a support system that propels us forward.

These connections not only provide invaluable advice, but they also serve as reminders that we are not alone in our quest for personal and professional development.

In conclusion, this subchapter emphasized the transformative power of embracing change and growth in the workplace. It reminded readers that change is not something to be feared, but rather something to be embraced with open arms. By letting go of fear, nurturing a thirst for learning and growth, and seeking support along the way, we can navigate career transitions and pursue personal and professional development with confidence and purpose. Life is a constant journey of change, and it is through embracing and harnessing that change that we find true fulfillment and success.

6

Business Relationships

Evaluating Partnership Compatibility

This subchapter in my book, "When It's Over," delves into the process of evaluating partnership compatibility in business relationships. It aims to provide insights not only on recognizing the signs that a partnership is no longer beneficial but also on how to navigate the complex terrain of dissolution with grace and integrity.

When evaluating partnership compatibility, I have discovered that there are certain key factors to consider. Firstly, it is essential to assess whether the values and goals of the partners are still aligned. As individuals and businesses evolve, their objectives and values can change, leading to a misalignment that can hinder progress. It is crucial to have open and honest conversations with one's partners to gauge their commitment and see if their vision still aligns with yours.

Another significant aspect to evaluate is the level of mutual trust and respect within the partnership. Without trust and respect, a partnership's foundation becomes shaky, making it difficult to foster a healthy and collaborative environment. It is important to evaluate whether these fundamental elements exist and if they can still be nurtured or if they have been irreparably damaged.

Furthermore, the financial aspect of a partnership cannot be overlooked. Evaluating the financial viability of the partnership is essential to ensure both parties are benefiting from the association. If one partner consistently bears a disproportionate burden, it can lead to resentment and strain the relationship. Careful evaluation of the financial contributions and gains helps to maintain balance and harmony within the partnership.

Additionally, the willingness and ability to communicate effectively become vital elements in determining partnership compatibility. Effective communication facilitates the smooth flow of ideas, addresses conflicts amicably, and strengthens trust. If communication breakdowns persist and efforts to resolve them prove futile, it may be a clear indication that the partnership has grown apart and dissolution could be the healthiest option.

As I reflect upon my own experiences in evaluating partnership compatibility, I recognize the importance of discernment and foresight. It is not always easy to admit that a partnership may no longer be beneficial, especially when emotions and history are involved. However, acknowledging the signs and initiating a graceful dissolution can lead to new opportunities for growth and success.

In the next section of this subchapter, I will delve deeper into the process of gracefully dissolving a partnership. I will share my personal experiences and research-backed insights on how to navigate this delicate process while preserving both personal and professional integrity. The dissolution of a partnership may be the end of one chapter, but with the right approach, it can also mark the beginning of a new and promising future.

Addressing Conflict and Misalignment

Conflict, like a tempest brewed from contrasting perspectives and desires, is an inherent part of life. In the confines of the business world, where ambitions intertwine and objectives clash, conflict becomes an indispensable companion. Yet, it is how we handle this companion that defines the outcome of our journey. For within every conflict lies an opportunity for growth and transformation.

The path to addressing conflict and misalignment begins with recognizing the underlying issues. It is not enough to merely acknowledge the surface-level disagreements; instead, we must delve deeper to unearth the roots of the conflict. We must unravel the intricate tapestry of emotions, past experiences, and unmet expectations that contribute to its existence. Only then can we hope to truly understand each other and forge a bridge of empathy.

Building upon this foundation of understanding, effective communication becomes the beacon that guides us towards resolution. I have come to realize that clear and compassionate communication holds the power to bridge the widest of divides. It is a dance of words and emotions, where listening with intent becomes just as vital as speaking with clarity. By actively seeking to understand the perspectives of others, we foster an environment that encourages open dialogue, trust, and collaboration. And it is through this shared understanding that we can begin to craft solutions that honor the needs and aspirations of all parties involved.

However, oftentimes conflict lingers beyond the realms of simple misunderstandings. It can manifest as a misalignment in values, goals, or working styles. In such instances, it becomes essential to address this misalignment head-on, acknowledging that not every partnership can be salvaged nor every disagreement resolved. Sometimes, the path to growth lies in accepting our differences and recognizing when it is time to part ways.

Nevertheless, when we are committed to addressing conflict and misalignment, it is wise to equip ourselves with an array of conflict resolution strategies. These approaches, like tools in a well-appointed toolkit, can aid in navigating the tumultuous terrain of conflict. From negotiations and compromises to meditation and seeking unbiased perspectives, the possibilities are as multifaceted as the conflicts themselves. The key lies in choosing the right strategy for each unique situation, employing it with humility and respect, and always keeping our sights set on a resolution that breeds growth and prosperity.

As we delve into the world of addressing conflict and misalignment, let us remember that conflict need not be viewed as an adversary to be defeated, but rather as an opportunity for growth and transformation. In the realm of business relationships, conflict is an ever-present companion, challenging us to rise above our differences and embrace the power of collaboration. By fostering effective communication and embracing conflict resolution strategies, we can transform these challenges into stepping stones towards success. So let us embark on this journey, with open hearts and minds, ready to navigate the complexities of conflict and emerge stronger on the other side.

Rebuilding Trust and Collaboration

With a steaming cup of coffee in hand, I delved into the depths of research on the topic. My desk was cluttered with journals, books, and articles, each one holding the key to understanding the intricate web of trust and collaboration in the business world. Struggling to navigate the extensive library of information, I felt overwhelmed. How could I distill this wealth of knowledge into a concise and meaningful subchapter?

Taking a deep breath, I began to unravel the problem. Trust, once broken, is like a fragile glass that shatters into a thousand irreparable pieces. Collaboration, once hindered, becomes a delicate dance of cautious steps. Repairing these fractured aspects of business relationships required more than just a temporary fix - it demanded a commitment to fundamental change.

In my exploration of the research, one concept stood out: communication. It seemed to be at the heart of rebuilding trust and collaboration. Effective communication was the glue that would bind fractured partnerships back together. I scribbled notes furiously, my pen racing across the page as I compiled the essential elements necessary for fostering a healthy working environment.

Listening, I discovered, was a pivotal skill that needed to be honed. Nurturing an environment where individuals felt heard and validated was the foundation for rebuilding trust. I pondered the significance of actively engaging in dialogue, acknowledging the concerns and perspectives of each party involved. It was crucial to facilitate an open exchange of ideas, fostering an atmosphere of mutual understanding.

Yet, communication alone was insufficient. Trust and collaboration required more than just words; they demanded action. Hence, I delved further into the research, seeking strategies to transform intentions into reality. Rebuilding trust meant demonstrating reliability, consistency, and integrity. I unraveled the complexities of empathy, recognizing its power in fostering understanding and building connections.

Collaboration, on the other hand, necessitated a conscious effort to cultivate an environment of trust. Collaboration meant letting go of personal agendas, embracing diversity, and recognizing the unique strengths that each team member brought to the table. It required vulnerability, an openness to new ideas, and a shared commitment to a common goal.

With these insights, I began to lay the foundation for a roadmap to rebuilding trust and collaboration. The subchapter would provide guidance, not only on repairing damaged partnerships but also on fostering an environment built on respect, empathy, and communication. It was a daunting task, but one that was essential if businesses were to thrive in a world governed by human connections.

As the words flowed from my pen onto the page, a sense of purpose enveloped me. This subchapter would serve as a beacon of hope for those grappling with fractured business relationships. It would guide them towards a path of healing, collaboration, and success. I was embarking on a journey to redefine trust and collaboration, and this subchapter would be the first step towards a better tomorrow.

Knowing When to Exit

As I sit down to write this subchapter, I can't help but feel a sense of urgency. It's a topic that holds great significance to me personally, as I have experienced the ups and downs of business relationships firsthand. There is a delicate balance between holding on and knowing when to let go. It requires a keen awareness of subtle signs, an openness to change, and the courage to venture into uncharted territories.

When I reflect on my past business relationships, I recall moments when doubts would creep in – a nagging feeling in the pit of my stomach telling me that something wasn't quite right. It started as a whisper, barely audible, but as time went on, it grew louder. It was in those moments that I needed to pause, to pay attention to the indicators that suggested it was time to exit.

One of the most crucial indicators is a lack of alignment in values and long-term goals. It's easy to overlook this aspect in the initial stages of a partnership, as excitement and enthusiasm often overshadow potential differences. However, as time goes on, these misalignments become more apparent and can lead to disharmony and conflict. When values clash and goals diverge, it becomes increasingly challenging to work together towards a common vision. Recognizing this misalignment early on can save us from investing valuable time and resources into a relationship that will eventually crumble under the weight of its inherent differences.

Another indicator that it may be time to exit a business relationship is a consistent lack of mutual respect. In the fast-paced world of business, it's easy to get caught up in the pursuit of success and forget the importance of treating others with dignity and respect. However, when respect is absent, the partnership becomes a toxic environment that stifles creativity, collaboration, and growth. When we find ourselves in a relationship where disrespect is the norm rather than the exception, it's crucial to question whether it's worth continuing on this path. No amount of success can justify sacrificing our self-worth and happiness.

Additionally, an indicator that often goes unnoticed is a stagnant or declining professional growth. Business relationships should be dynamic and provide opportunities for learning and advancement. However, when we find ourselves stuck in a rut, where growth and progress have become stagnant or even regressive, it's time to evaluate the viability of that relationship. We must question whether this partnership is still aligned with our personal and professional aspirations. If it inhibits our growth rather than foster it, it's a sure sign that it's time to move on.

Making the decision to exit a business relationship is never easy. It requires a deep introspection, a willingness to let go of familiarity, and the determination to seek new opportunities. It's a moment of truth where we confront our fears and step into the unknown. But it is in those moments of uncertainty that we discover our true potential and pave the way for new beginnings. Knowing when to exit is not a sign of failure, but rather a sign of wisdom and strength. It is a testament to our ability to adapt, grow, and pursue our dreams with unwavering determination.

In the following pages, we will explore strategies to make informed decisions when the time comes to exit a business relationship. We'll delve into the power of intuition, the importance of seeking counsel, and the steps required to embark on a new path. Until then, take a moment to reflect on your own experiences and consider whether there are any indicators suggesting it's time to exit a business relationship. Remember, life is a series of choices, and knowing when to exit can open the door to new opportunities beyond your wildest dreams.

Learning and Growing from Experiences

As I reflect on the many twists and turns of my journey in the world of business relationships, it becomes clear that each experience has been woven into the fabric of my growth. The ups and downs, the triumphs and setbacks, have all served as catalysts for my personal and professional development. In this subchapter, I seek to delve into the lessons I have learned and share with my readers inspiration and guidance on how to apply these lessons to future endeavors.

Every business relationship, whether prosperous or fraught with challenges, offers an opportunity for growth. It is crucial to fully immerse ourselves in the experience, extracting the valuable nuggets of wisdom hidden within. This process begins with self-reflection, a willingness to admit personal flaws and areas in need of improvement. It is through this humility that we uncover the lessons that will shape our future success.

One of the most profound lessons I have learned is the importance of effective communication. In the fast-paced world of business, miscommunication can lead to detrimental consequences. Reflecting on my past experiences, I recognize key moments where a lack of clear and concise communication resulted in missed opportunities or strained relationships. These instances have taught me to prioritize active listening, to ask questions when in doubt, and to always clarify expectations. By embodying these principles, we can foster stronger and more collaborative business relationships.

Another lesson that has left an indelible mark on my journey is the power of adaptability. The business landscape is constantly evolving, and the ability to adapt to change is imperative for success. Reflecting on my own experiences, I recall instances where I resisted change, clinging stubbornly to outdated methods and practices. It was through embracing the unknown, however, that I discovered new perspectives, innovative strategies, and unforeseen opportunities. I encourage my readers to recognize the value in stepping outside of their comfort zones, to embrace change as an opportunity for growth rather than a threat to familiarity.

Integrity and ethical behavior are essential pillars upon which to build strong business relationships. In a world often clouded by deceit and dishonesty, maintaining an unwavering commitment to authenticity and moral principles is a rarity. Through my own experiences, I have witnessed the power of integrity in forging enduring partnerships and earning the trust of clients and colleagues alike. I encourage my readers to navigate the complex realm of business with integrity as their compass, for it is through this adherence to ethical conduct that we can establish reputations steeped in trust and respect.

In conclusion, the rich tapestry of our business relationship experiences offers invaluable lessons. This subchapter serves not only as an exploration of these lessons but as an inspiration for readers to embrace them and apply them to their own future endeavors. By prioritizing effective communication, adaptability, and integrity, we lay the groundwork for fruitful professional relationships and lasting success. As we navigate the intricate web of the business world, let us be guided by the wisdom gained from our experiences, for it is in learning and growing that we truly thrive.

7

∽

Overcoming Hardships

Navigating Grief and Loss

Grief is a heavy and complex emotion that washes over us when we experience the loss of someone dear to us or the end of a significant relationship in our lives. It can strike with the force of a tidal wave, leaving us gasping for air and struggling to find solid ground. I remember the day my relationship ended with Emily, the feeling of my world crumbling around me, and the overwhelming waves of grief crashing over me. It was as if I had lost a piece of myself, and I was left grappling with the weight of emptiness and sorrow.

In the midst of my grief, I found solace in understanding the process of navigating through it. The first step was accepting the reality of the loss. Denial can be a tempting friend, shielding us from the harsh truth of our circumstances. But it is only through acknowledging the end of a relationship that we can begin to move forward. For me, this meant allowing myself to feel the raw emotions that surfaced, rather than burying them deep within. It was a painful journey, but it was one that needed to be taken.

Once I acknowledged the reality of the loss, I embarked on a path of healing. Healing from grief requires patience and self-compassion. It is not a linear journey, but rather a series of ups and downs, twists and turns. There were days when I felt like I was making progress, and others when I felt like I was back at square one. It was crucial to remind myself that grief takes time, and it is okay to have setbacks along the way.

During this healing process, I discovered the importance of healthy coping mechanisms. Engaging in activities that bring us joy and provide a sense of comfort can help ease the pain of grief. For me, writing became a lifeline. It allowed me to express my emotions and make sense of the whirlwind of thoughts in my mind. I also found solace in nature, taking long walks by the river and allowing the beauty of the world to soothe my aching heart. Each person will have their own unique coping mechanisms, but the key is to find what brings you a sense of peace and solace.

While finding solace in personal coping mechanisms is vital, it is equally essential to seek support from others. Grief can be isolating, causing us to retreat into ourselves. However, it is through the support of others that we can find strength and navigate our way through the darkest of times. Seeking the guidance of a therapist or joining a support group can provide a safe space to share our experiences and lean on the empathy of others who have walked similar paths. By allowing ourselves to be vulnerable and open to the support of others, we create a network of healing that helps to carry us through the toughest moments.

Navigating grief and loss is a deeply personal journey, unique to each individual. It is a process that demands self-compassion, patience, and the willingness to embrace both the highs and lows that come with healing. From accepting the reality of the loss to finding healthy coping mechanisms and seeking support, this journey is one of self-discovery and growth. As I continue to navigate my own grief, I hold onto the hope that, one day, the weight of loss will be lighter, and the sun will shine brightly once more.

Cultivating Self-Compassion

I believe that self-compassion is a powerful antidote for the wounds we carry deep within ourselves. It is a gentle reminder that we are worthy of love and care, especially during the most difficult periods of our lives. Instead of berating ourselves for our shortcomings or dwelling on past mistakes, we must learn to embrace our own imperfections with warmth and acceptance.

But how do we go about cultivating self-compassion? It starts with recognizing that we are not alone in our struggles. We are human beings, and it is natural for us to face challenges and experience pain. By acknowledging our shared humanity, we can begin to let go of the shame and self-judgment that often weighs us down.

Another crucial aspect of cultivating self-compassion is practicing self-care. This means taking the time to engage in activities that nourish our souls and replenish our energy. Whether it's a long, relaxing bath or a walk in nature, finding moments to tune into ourselves and tend to our needs is essential. It's about prioritizing ourselves and giving ourselves permission to heal.

Furthermore, as we embark on the path of self-compassion, it is indispensable to become aware of our inner dialogue. Our thoughts and self-talk can either be our greatest ally or our harshest critic. In challenging times, it is important to speak to ourselves with kindness and understanding, just as we would to a dear friend who is going through a difficult situation. Reframing negative or self-deprecating thoughts into more compassionate and empowering ones can have a profound impact on our emotional well-being.

Mastering self-compassion is a journey that cannot be rushed. It demands unwavering commitment, endurance, and unwavering focus. Nonetheless, the rewards that await us at the end of this arduous path are immeasurable. By dedicating ourselves to cultivating self-compassion, we bestow upon ourselves the invaluable gift of solace and encouragement in our bleakest moments—reminding ourselves that we are innately deserving of affection and benevolence, even when the world appears to have abandoned us.

In the upcoming chapters, I will divulge precise and effective strategies, along with practical exercises, that will enable you to deepen your practice of self-compassion. These indispensable tools will serve as your guiding light as you nurture and mend your inner being, allowing you to navigate through life's harshest trials with composure and fortitude.

Remember, the expedition towards self-compassion commences at this very moment, and I pledge to accompany you every step of the way. Together, we shall unravel the intricate layers of self-doubt and unearth the limitless reservoir of love and compassion that resides within each and every one of us.

Embracing Personal Growth

Reflecting on the past is an essential step in embracing personal growth. It allows you to gain a better understanding of what went wrong and why the relationship ended. Instead of dwelling on the pain, I found solace in reflecting on the lessons I learned throughout the journey. It was not an easy process, as it forced me to confront my own shortcomings and accept my share of responsibility for the end of the relationship.

During this period of reflection, I immersed myself in self-exploration. I took the time to evaluate my own actions, thoughts, and behaviors. I questioned the choices I made and how they influenced the relationship. I dove deep into my core values and examined if they were truly aligned with the person I aspired to be. This introspection allowed me to develop a newfound sense of self-awareness.

Learning from the past is the next crucial step in personal growth. Every relationship teaches us valuable lessons, even the ones that end in heartbreak. As painful as it may be, it is essential to extract the wisdom buried within those experiences. By analyzing my own behavior, as well as the dynamics of the relationship, I was able to identify patterns and red flags that I had previously overlooked. This newfound understanding served as a blueprint for my personal growth journey, enabling me to make better choices in future relationships.

I delved into extensive research on relationship psychology and self-improvement to further enhance my understanding. The studies I came across revealed fascinating insights into the dynamics of love, attachment, and personal development. They highlighted the significance of self-love, setting healthy boundaries, and cultivating a growth mindset. Armed with this knowledge, I embarked on a journey of intentional personal growth.

Evolution is the ultimate goal of embracing personal growth after the end of a relationship. It is about transforming the pain into strength, the heartache into resilience. I learned to let go of the past and trust that it was merely a stepping stone towards a better future. As I embraced personal growth, I became more compassionate towards myself and others. I began to see the beauty in imperfection and appreciate the growth that comes from vulnerability.

This journey of embracing personal growth was not without its setbacks and challenges. There were times when I stumbled and fell, questioning if I had made any progress at all. There were moments of doubt and loneliness, when it felt easier to revert to old patterns rather than forging a new path. However, with each setback, I persisted. I reminded myself that personal growth is not a linear process, but rather a journey with ups and downs.

Today, I stand here, a testament to the power of embracing personal growth after the end of a relationship. I have emerged from the shadows of heartbreak and transformed into a stronger, wiser version of myself. I have learned to love and embrace my flaws, recognizing that they are merely a part of my unique journey. I am no longer defined by the end of a relationship; instead, I am defined by the growth that emerged from it.

In conclusion, when a relationship comes to an end, it is an invitation for personal growth. By reflecting on the past, learning from mistakes, and evolving, we can transform heartbreak into an opportunity for self-discovery. It is a chance to rewrite our narrative, reclaim our identity, and embrace the beauty of personal growth. Let us not shy away from the pain, but instead, let it be the catalyst for our evolution.

Seeking Professional Support

When my world came crashing down, I found myself lost in a sea of emotions. The pain was unbearable, and I felt like I had hit rock bottom. I needed help, someone who could guide me through the darkness and help me find my way back to the light. That's when I turned to professional support.

I knew that seeking professional help was not a sign of weakness, but rather an act of bravery. I recognized that I needed someone with the knowledge and experience to help me navigate the treacherous waters of healing. And so, I began my search for a therapist, counselor, or coach who could offer me guidance and healing.

The first step was researching different professionals in my area. I wanted someone who specialized in the type of support I needed, someone who had experience working with individuals going through similar transitions. I read countless testimonials and reviews, searching for someone who resonated with me.

After narrowing down my options, I reached out for initial consultations. These introductory sessions allowed me to get a sense of the therapist's style and see if we could establish a connection. It was important to find someone I felt comfortable opening up to, someone who would create a safe space for me to share my deepest fears and vulnerabilities.

Throughout my journey, I discovered that professional support offered numerous benefits. For one, it provided me with a non-judgmental space to express my emotions and thoughts without fear of being misunderstood. Having someone genuinely listen to my struggles and validate my experiences was incredibly therapeutic.

Additionally, the guidance and expertise of a professional helped me gain new perspectives on my situation. They offered insights and techniques that I had never considered before, helping me navigate my feelings and reactions more effectively. They provided me with coping strategies, mindfulness exercises, and tools to rebuild my shattered self-esteem.

Furthermore, seeking professional support provided me with a sense of accountability. Knowing that I had someone who cared about my progress and believed in my ability to heal motivated me to stay committed to my journey. It wasn't always easy, but having someone to lean on during the tough times made a world of difference.

Finding professional support was not a quick fix or a magic solution, but rather a vital component in my healing process. It was like having a trusted companion by my side as I braved the storm. Together, we unraveled the layers of pain, explored the depths of my emotions, and worked towards rebuilding a stronger and more resilient version of myself.

If you find yourself navigating a difficult transition, remember that seeking professional support is not a sign of weakness, but rather an act of self-care and self-love. Having someone with the knowledge, experience, and empathy to guide you through the challenging times can make all the difference. So, take the leap and reach out to find the compassionate professional who will help you find your way to a brighter tomorrow.

Moving Forward with Resilience

When I found myself at the end of a tumultuous relationship, I felt completely defeated. The pain was overwhelming, and I questioned whether I would ever be able to pick up the pieces and move forward. But I soon realized that resilience is a powerful force, capable of propelling us towards a brighter future.

The first step in moving forward with resilience is accepting the end of the relationship. It can be tempting to dwell on what went wrong or to cling to memories of happier times, but this only prolongs the healing process. Instead, I found solace in accepting the reality of the situation and acknowledging that the relationship had served its purpose, even if that purpose was simply to teach me valuable life lessons.

Once we accept the end of the relationship, it's important to give ourselves permission to grieve. It's okay to feel sad, angry, or lost. These emotions are a natural part of the healing process. I allowed myself to cry, to scream, and to feel every wave of pain that washed over me. And in doing so, I discovered the strength that comes from allowing ourselves to fully experience our emotions.

After the initial wave of grief subsided, I began to focus on rebuilding my life. I realized that my identity was not defined solely by my relationship status. I had dreams, passions, and aspirations that were waiting to be rediscovered. I decided to embrace the opportunity for new beginnings and create a life that was authentically mine.

Finding a support system is crucial in moving forward with resilience. Whether it be friends, family, or a therapist, having people to lean on during this difficult time can make all the difference. I sought out individuals who had faced similar challenges and could offer guidance and support. Their shared experiences provided me with hope and reassurance that I too could overcome the pain and create a fulfilling life.

Lastly, I learned to cultivate a sense of gratitude. Even in the darkest of moments, there is always something to be grateful for. I made it a daily practice to acknowledge the small blessings in my life – from a beautiful sunrise to a warm cup of coffee. This practice not only helped shift my mindset towards an attitude of gratitude, but it also reminded me that there is beauty and joy to be found in every day, no matter the circumstances.

As I look back on my journey of moving forward with resilience, I am grateful for the opportunity to grow and evolve. I have learned that the end of a relationship does not mean the end of happiness or the prospect of love. It simply signifies a new chapter, filled with infinite possibilities.

So, dear readers, take this opportunity to embrace your own journey of resilience. Allow yourself to grieve, to rediscover your passions, to lean on your support system, and to cultivate gratitude. In doing so, you will find the strength to create a life that is not only fulfilling but also filled with hope and endless possibilities. Remember, the end of a relationship is not the end of your story – it is merely the beginning of a new and extraordinary chapter. Embrace it with open arms and move forward with resilience.

8

Becoming a Better Person

Self-Reflection and Awareness

In the tumultuous journey of personal growth, one profound realization that I have come to is the vital importance of self-reflection and self-awareness. This subchapter aims to shed light on the significance of these introspective practices and provide exercises and guidance on how we can develop a deeper understanding of ourselves.

Our society often focuses on external achievements and material possessions as the markers of success. However, true fulfillment and growth lie within us, waiting to be explored and understood. As the saying goes, "Know thyself," and this is where self-reflection becomes the compass guiding us on our path.

In the beginning, self-reflection may seem daunting, as it involves peering into the depths of our thoughts, emotions, and actions. It requires us to confront our fears, failures, and vulnerabilities head-on. Nonetheless, it is within this soul-searching process that we discover profound insights and gain clarity about our true desires, values, and purpose.

To embark on the journey of self-reflection, it is essential to create a nurturing and safe space conducive to introspection. Carve out dedicated time in your daily routine, away from distractions, to delve into the depths of your soul. Find a quiet corner, light a candle, or play soothing music to set the mood for introspection.

One exercise that has helped me immensely is journaling. Writing down my thoughts, emotions, and experiences allows me to observe patterns, gain perspective, and identify areas in need of growth. When pouring yourself onto the pages of a journal, there are no judgments or boundaries. It becomes a sacred space where your deepest reflections can emerge.

Another powerful technique is meditation. Through the practice of mindfulness, we learn to observe our thoughts and emotions without attachment or judgment. As we sit in stillness, our mind becomes a clear pool reflecting the vast landscape of our inner world. This practice cultivates self-awareness and enables us to gain insights into our patterns of thinking and reacting.

Additionally, seeking feedback from trusted friends, mentors, or therapists can provide invaluable perspectives that we might otherwise miss. These individuals can serve as compassionate mirrors, reflecting back to us aspects of ourselves that may be hidden or obscured. Remember, it takes courage to ask for feedback, but the insights gained can be transformative.

As we deepen our self-reflection and self-awareness, we unlock a myriad of benefits. We gain a better understanding of our strengths, weaknesses, and limitations, allowing us to make intentional choices aligned with our true essence. Self-acceptance blooms, leading to increased self-confidence and an unwavering belief in our ability to navigate life's challenges.

Moreover, self-reflection opens the doors to empathy and compassion towards ourselves and others. As we explore our own inner landscape, we cultivate a deeper understanding of the complexities of the human experience. This newfound empathy strengthens our relationships, fosters connection, and promotes harmony within our communities.

In conclusion, self-reflection and self-awareness are indispensable tools in the pursuit of personal growth and fulfillment. Through dedicated practices such as journaling, meditation, and seeking feedback, we can develop a profound understanding of ourselves. In this process, we uncover our true desires, values, and purpose, allowing us to live authentically and align with our highest potential. Embrace the power of self-reflection, for it is the gateway to a life of genuine self-discovery and profound transformation.

Building Healthy Boundaries

As I sit down to write about building healthy boundaries, memories flood my mind. Growing up in a small town called Willowbrook, I had never truly understood the importance of setting boundaries until my life took an unexpected turn. My name is Dakota Frandsen, and I have journeyed through various relationships, both romantic and platonic, realizing the essence of boundaries along the way.

Boundaries are not just lines we draw; they are the backbone of healthy connections. We often find ourselves entangled in relationships that leave us feeling overwhelmed, drained, or manipulated, simply because we fail to establish and maintain solid boundaries. Little did I know that learning how to set these boundaries would transform not just my relationships but also my own well-being.

Reflecting upon my experiences, I realized that boundaries serve as a means of self-care and protection. They act as a shield against emotional and psychological harm, allowing both parties involved to foster a healthier connection. Without boundaries, relationships become a tangled web of confusion, where personal limits are blurred, and trust gradually erodes.

So, how do we go about building these crucial boundaries? I believe it starts with self-awareness and knowing our emotional limits. It requires us to understand our needs, values, and personal space. From there, we can establish clear communication and express our boundaries to those around us. It may seem daunting at first, but it's a necessary step towards cultivating healthy connections.

One technique I have found useful is the art of assertive communication. Rather than passively allowing boundaries to be crossed or aggressively lashing out, assertiveness allows us to voice our needs and concerns in a respectful manner. By affirming our values and asserting our rights, we create an atmosphere of mutual respect and understanding.

However, setting boundaries is just the beginning. Maintaining them requires consistency and self-discipline. It can be difficult at times, especially when we fear confrontation or worry about offending others. But we must remember that our well-being is just as important as anyone else's, and a healthy relationship is built upon mutual respect for each other's boundaries.

It's also crucial to remember that boundaries are not meant to isolate or push others away. Rather, they allow us to establish a solid foundation for connection, where both parties can thrive as individuals while simultaneously building a harmonious relationship. It's about finding a balance between personal boundaries and open communication, creating a space where everyone involved feels valued and respected.

In this subchapter, we will delve deeper into the significance of building healthy boundaries in all relationships. We will explore real-life experiences, case studies, and expert research to provide practical tips and techniques for establishing and maintaining boundaries. Let us embark on this journey together, as we uncover the transformative power of building healthy boundaries, paving the way for fulfilling and mutually satisfying connections.

Cultivating Self-Love and Self-Care

Step 1: Recognizing the Importance of Self-Love

As I embarked on my journey of self-discovery, I realized that self-love is not just an abstract concept but a fundamental pillar of our existence. It is about acknowledging our worth and embracing ourselves for who we truly are. For far too long, I had neglected my own needs, believing that taking care of others was more important. But the truth is, if we don't love and care for ourselves, how can we be truly available for others?

Step 2: Embracing Imperfection

One of the most transformative moments in my life occurred when I decided to embrace my imperfections. I realized that striving for perfection was not only exhausting but also detrimental to my well-being. Instead, I began to see beauty in my quirks, flaws, and the unique tapestry of my own story. Self-love means accepting ourselves unconditionally, including our imperfections, and understanding that they make us who we are.

Step 3: Setting Boundaries

Learning to set boundaries was a critical component of my journey towards self-love and self-care. I realized that I had allowed others to take advantage of my kindness, leaving me depleted and drained. By setting healthy boundaries, I took control of my own emotional well-being. This meant saying no when necessary, prioritizing my own needs, and recognizing that my happiness was just as important as anyone else's.

Step 4: Nurturing our Physical and Emotional Well-being

Taking care of our physical and emotional well-being is an absolute necessity when it comes to self-care. I discovered the power in consistently engaging in activities that brought me joy – whether it was practicing yoga, going for long walks in nature, or indulging in a good book. Prioritizing self-care practices not only replenishes our energy but also allows us to show up fully in our personal and professional lives.

Step 5: Surrounding Ourselves with Positive Influences

The people we surround ourselves with have a profound impact on our self-love journey. In my case, I was fortunate to have a supportive circle of friends and family who uplifted and encouraged me. They reminded me of my worth and helped me see my own potential. Surrounding ourselves with positive influences allows us to cultivate an environment that fosters self-love and personal growth.

Step 6: Practicing Gratitude

Practicing gratitude became an integral part of my self-love journey. This simple yet powerful practice helped me shift my focus from what I lacked to what I already had. I started keeping a gratitude journal, writing down three things I was grateful for every day. By acknowledging the blessings in my life, I developed a deeper sense of appreciation and contentment, cultivating self-love for both the present and the future.

Step 7: Celebrating Small Wins

We often forget to celebrate our progress, no matter how small. This subchapter reminds us to acknowledge and celebrate our achievements along the way. From reaching personal goals to overcoming obstacles, each small win should be recognized and celebrated. By doing so, we reinforce our self-love and motivation to keep moving forward.

In conclusion, cultivating self-love and self-care is an ongoing process that requires dedication and commitment. It is about recognizing our worth, embracing our imperfections, setting boundaries, nurturing our physical and emotional well-being, surrounding ourselves with positive influences, practicing gratitude, and celebrating our small wins. With each step we take, we inch closer to personal growth and a deeper, more meaningful connection with ourselves.

Building Meaningful Connections

When a relationship comes to an end, it can be an incredibly challenging and painful experience. The void left by the absence of a once cherished partnership can leave one feeling lost, unsure of how to move forward. In these moments, it becomes imperative to reconnect with oneself and rediscover the joy and fulfillment that can come from building meaningful connections with others.

As I embarked on my own journey of rebuilding after a heart-shattering breakup, I discovered that building meaningful connections goes beyond simply seeking out companionship. It is about delving deep within ourselves and understanding our own desires, strengths, and vulnerabilities. Only through this process of self-reflection can we attract compatible and healthy relationships.

One aspect that became evident during my exploration was the importance of knowing what I truly wanted in a relationship. It was crucial to identify the qualities and values that aligned with my own, which laid the foundation for a meaningful connection. I genuinely craved a partner who would support and encourage me, someone who would challenge and inspire me to become the best version of myself. For this reason, it was vital to take the time to reflect on my own aspirations and desires, helping me to recognize potential partners who shared those same values.

Nurturing these connections, once established, also requires a high level of emotional intelligence and communication. It is essential to create a safe space for vulnerability and express oneself authentically. In my own experience, I found that open and honest conversations allowed for a deeper understanding and connection with my partner. By fostering an environment built on trust and mutual respect, I was able to develop a bond that went far beyond surface-level interaction.

Another key aspect of building meaningful connections is understanding that relationships require effort and investment. It is not enough to simply find someone who checks all the boxes on our list of desired qualities. We must actively participate in the growth and development of the connection, continuously nourishing it with love, understanding, and empathy. This means being present, actively listening, and showing genuine interest in our partner's experiences and emotions.

Throughout my journey, I came to understand that building meaningful connections after the end of a relationship is not an overnight process. It requires patience, self-reflection, and a willingness to learn from past experiences. By attracting and nurturing healthy relationships, we create a foundation upon which growth, love, and fulfillment can flourish.

As I continued on this path, I realized that building meaningful connections goes beyond the realm of romantic relationships. It is about fostering connections with friends, family members, and even within our professional lives. By building these meaningful connections, we create a support system that sustains us and enriches our lives.

In conclusion, the process of building meaningful connections after the end of relationships is a deeply personal journey. It involves self-reflection, understanding one's desires, and investing time and effort into nurturing those connections. By approaching new relationships with authenticity, emotional intelligence, and a commitment to growth, we can attract and build relationships that bring joy and fulfillment into our lives.

Finding Happiness Within

The struggle to find happiness can often feel like an elusive quest. We tirelessly search for external factors to bring us joy, believing that a fulfilling life lies outside of ourselves. But what if the key to true happiness is actually found within?

I have spent much of my life chasing happiness in all the wrong places. I sought validation from others, desperately seeking their approval and acceptance. I pursued material possessions, believing that acquiring more things would bring me lasting contentment. But the more I chased after external sources of happiness, the more I realized that they were merely temporary fixes, leaving me feeling empty and unfulfilled.

It wasn't until I embarked on a journey of self-discovery that I began to understand that the path to true happiness starts within. I started by shifting my focus inward, acknowledging and accepting my emotions, flaws, and strengths. I learned to cultivate self-compassion, treating myself with the same kindness and understanding that I would offer a dear friend.

Through this process, I discovered the importance of self-fulfillment. It is not about conforming to societal expectations or adhering to someone else's definition of success. Instead, it is about recognizing and nurturing our own unique talents, passions, and desires. It is about aligning our lives with our truest selves and finding purpose in the pursuit of our dreams.

To create a joyful and purposeful life, we must first identify what truly brings us joy. This requires introspection and self-reflection. What activities or hobbies make our hearts sing? What gives us a sense of purpose and fulfillment? By asking ourselves these questions and exploring different avenues, we can uncover our passions and rediscover our inner sense of joy.

But finding happiness within is not just about discovering our own personal bliss. It is also about learning to embrace the present moment and find contentment in the simple pleasures of life. This involves cultivating gratitude for what we already have and finding joy in the smallest of things, whether it's the warmth of a cup of tea, the beauty of a sunset, or a heartfelt conversation with a loved one.

Creating a joyful and purposeful life also requires a shift in mindset. We must let go of limiting beliefs and embrace a mindset of abundance and possibility. It is about reframing challenges as opportunities for growth and viewing setbacks as stepping stones to success. By adopting a positive mindset and choosing to focus on the good in our lives, we can cultivate a greater sense of happiness and fulfillment.

In the pursuit of self-fulfillment, it is important to remember that the journey is ongoing. Happiness is not a destination but rather a constant process of learning, growing, and evolving. It requires a commitment to ourselves, a dedication to continuously nurturing our own well-being and pursuing what brings us true joy.

So, dear reader, I invite you to embark on this journey of self-discovery with an open heart and an open mind. Embrace the idea that true happiness lies within you, waiting to be discovered. Nurture your passions, embrace the present moment, and cultivate a positive mindset. In doing so, you will find not only happiness but also a sense of purpose and fulfillment that will guide you to live a truly meaningful life.

9

∿

Embracing Change

The Power of Change

Change is a force that, more often than not, we resist. We find solace in the familiar, the routine, and the predictable. It is this fear of the unknown that often holds us back from personal growth and transformation. But what if I told you that change, when embraced, has the power to bring unimaginable possibilities into our lives?

I used to be a creature of habit. My days were meticulously planned, my routines etched into my being. I found comfort in the monotony of life, believing that it offered stability and security. But deep down, I knew that something was missing. There was a fire within me, flickering ever so softly, yearning to break free from the chains that held it captive.

It wasn't until a series of unexpected events rocked my world that I realized the power of change. Life had thrown me into the depths of despair, leaving me shattered and questioning everything I once believed in. I was faced with a choice – succumb to the pain and stay within the confines of my comfort zone or embrace the turmoil and allow it to propel me forward.

I chose the latter.

It was not an easy path to tread. Change demanded that I step out of my comfort zone, confront my fears, and challenge the status quo. But with each step, I could feel myself shedding the layers of the person I once was, making way for the person I could become. It was a journey of self-discovery, a voyage into the uncharted territories of my own potential.

Embracing change meant embracing uncertainty. It meant being willing to let go of the familiar and venture into the unknown. It meant surrendering control and trusting the process, even when the path ahead seemed blurry. And through this surrender, I discovered that change is not something to be feared, but rather a catalyst for growth and transformation.

Change offered me new opportunities, ones I never could have imagined in my wildest dreams. It introduced me to new people, new ideas, and new perspectives that challenged my own beliefs and expanded my horizons. It pushed me to confront my weaknesses and embrace my strengths. It forced me to redefine who I was and what I was capable of.

Change allowed me to break free from the limitations I had unknowingly placed upon myself, opening doors that had long been closed. It invited me to rewrite my story, to create a narrative that was true to my authentic self. And in doing so, it empowered me to live a life that was not defined by circumstances, but rather by my ability to adapt, grow, and transform.

So, if you find yourself at a crossroads, afraid of the changes that lay ahead, I urge you to embrace them. Embrace the discomfort, the uncertainty, and the fear. Trust that within the chaos lies the opportunity for growth and self-discovery. Just as a caterpillar must endure the transformative process within its cocoon to emerge as a butterfly, so too must we embrace the power of change to unlock our true potential.

In the end, the choice is yours. Will you remain stagnant, clinging desperately to the familiar, or will you embrace the winds of change and let them carry you towards a future filled with new opportunities and endless possibilities? The power is in your hands. Embrace change and watch as it guides you towards the person you were always meant to be.

Navigating Life Transitions

Life transitions can manifest in various forms - a career change, the end of a relationship, moving to a new city, or even the loss of a loved one. Each transition carries its own unique set of challenges, forcing us to confront our fears and reevaluate our priorities. Whether the transition was self-imposed or thrust upon us, the adjustments required can often feel overwhelming. However, it is in these moments of discomfort and uncertainty that we have the opportunity to cultivate resilience and personal growth.

Navigating life transitions begins with acknowledging our emotions and allowing ourselves to feel the full spectrum of what arises within us. It is perfectly natural to experience a myriad of emotions during times of transition - from excitement and anticipation to fear and sadness. By acknowledging and honoring these emotions, we create space for healing and personal understanding. This emotional exploration acts as a compass, guiding us through the uncharted territory of change.

As we traverse the landscape of transition, it is crucial to cultivate a mindset of adaptability and flexibility. The ability to adjust our expectations and embrace the unknown is essential in finding stability during uncertain times. We must be willing to let go of the familiar, recognize the impermanence of life, and open ourselves up to new possibilities. Embracing change requires us to step out of our comfort zones, challenge self-limiting beliefs, and embrace the discomfort of growth.

Finding stability amidst the turbulence of life transitions can be achieved through the cultivation of self-care practices. Turning inward and prioritizing our well-being during times of change ensures we have the strength and resilience to navigate the challenges that lie ahead. Engaging in activities that nourish our mind, body, and soul allows us to maintain balance and perspective, even during the most tumultuous periods. Whether it be through meditation, journaling, exercise, or connecting with loved ones, self-care acts as a guiding light, illuminating our path towards stability and emotional grounding.

Furthermore, seeking support from our network of family, friends, or professionals can provide invaluable guidance and assistance during life transitions. Sharing our experiences, fears, and hopes with others fosters a sense of community, reminding us that we are not alone in our struggles. The wisdom and encouragement of others can offer insights and perspectives that we may not have considered, helping us navigate the complexities of our own transitions.

In the depths of life transitions, it is easy to succumb to feelings of hopelessness and surrender to the unknown. However, by embracing change with grace and resilience, we unlock the potential for profound personal growth. Navigating life transitions is a courageous and transformative act, allowing us to harness our inner strength and emerge stronger and wiser on the other side. So, dear readers, as you embark on this journey, remember to embrace your emotions, adapt with flexibility, prioritize self-care, and seek support. May these tools guide you through the labyrinth of life transitions, illuminating the path towards a brighter, more resilient future.

Embracing Uncertainty and Letting Go

In a world that constantly bombards us with expectations and pressures, it's easy to succumb to the illusion that we have control over every aspect of our lives. We meticulously plan and strategize, thinking that we can prevent any surprises from coming our way. But life is not a neatly written script; it's a chaotic masterpiece filled with unpredictable twists and turns. And while it's natural to desire stability and security, embracing the uncertainty can be liberating.

One of the strategies I discovered was the art of surrendering. Instead of resisting and fighting against the inevitable changes and uncertainties, I learned to surrender to the flow of life. It's like swimming against a powerful current; the more you struggle, the more exhausted you become. But when you surrender and allow the currents to guide you, you effortlessly glide through the waves. Surrendering doesn't mean giving up; it means trusting that everything will unfold as it should and having faith in the process.

Another technique I incorporated into my life was practicing mindfulness. By being fully present in the moment, I was able to let go of my attachment to outcomes and appreciate the beauty of uncertainty. Mindfulness taught me to observe my thoughts and feelings without judgment, allowing me to detach from the need for control. It provided me with the ability to embrace each moment as it came, without worrying about the past or being consumed by the future.

Letting go of control also involved relinquishing the need for certainty. I realized that the fear of the unknown stems from our desire for everything to be sure and certain. But the truth is, certainty is an illusion. Nothing in life is guaranteed, and instead of resisting this reality, it's important to welcome it. I learned to find comfort in the unknown, understanding that it is a canvas of endless possibilities and opportunities for growth.

The practice of embracing uncertainty and letting go of control is undoubtedly challenging. It requires courage and a willingness to release the grip we have on our lives. But as I gradually let go, I started to experience a newfound sense of freedom and peace. It was as if a weight had been lifted off my shoulders, and I could finally breathe again. Embracing uncertainty doesn't mean we abandon all responsibility; rather, it allows us to discover a balance between taking action and surrendering to the flow.

As I continued on my journey, I encountered moments of doubt and fear, but instead of being crippled by them, I used them as opportunities for growth. I realized that embracing uncertainty is not a one-time event but an ongoing process. It requires constant practice and self-reflection. And so, I promised myself that I would continue to nurture a mindset that embraces the unknown and finds solace in surrender.

In conclusion, embracing uncertainty and letting go of control is a transformative process that opens the door to a more fulfilling and peaceful life. By surrendering to the flow of life, practicing mindfulness, and embracing the beauty of the unknown, we can find freedom in relinquishing the need for certainty. It is through this journey that we learn to navigate the unpredictable waters of life with grace and resilience. So, let us embrace uncertainty, let go of control, and embrace the adventure that lies ahead.

Transforming Fear into Courage

To truly embody courage in the face of change, one must first understand the nature of fear. Fear, at its core, is a protective mechanism, an alarm system designed to keep us safe from potential harm. It is our mind's way of signaling that we are stepping into unfamiliar territory, a place fraught with unknown dangers. But what if we were to shift our perspective and view fear not as an enemy but as a catalyst for growth?

One vital strategy for transforming fear into courage is to acknowledge and embrace the resistance that accompanies change. Resistance stems from our natural inclination to seek comfort and stability, to cling to what is familiar. It is the voice in our head that whispers, "Stay where you are, it's safer here." But the truth is, growth and evolution lie beyond the boundaries of our comfort zone.

To overcome resistance, we must cultivate a mindset of openness and adaptability. We must remind ourselves that change brings with it new possibilities, opportunities that may lead us to uncharted territories. It is in this space of uncertainty that courage flourishes, where we see fear as a signpost, guiding us towards our highest potential.

Another strategy to transform fear into courage is to develop a support system. Surrounding ourselves with individuals who share similar aspirations and values can provide a sense of reassurance and encouragement. When we have someone by our side who understands our fears and challenges, their unwavering support becomes a source of strength and inspiration.

Moreover, it is essential to practice self-compassion and kindness during times of change. Often, fear brings with it an influx of self-doubt and criticism. We may question our abilities, our worthiness, and our capacity to navigate the unknown. By cultivating self-compassion, we offer ourselves the understanding and grace needed to embrace vulnerability and take courageous steps towards growth.

Lastly, utilizing visualization techniques can be a powerful tool in transforming fear into courage. By vividly imagining ourselves successfully navigating the changes that lie ahead, we create a sense of familiarity and confidence. Visualization allows us to rehearse our responses to potential challenges, equipping us with the mental fortitude necessary to face them head-on.

In this transformative journey, as we shed the shackles of fear, the cloak of courage envelops us, empowering us to embrace change with open arms. By implementing these strategies, we invite the unknown to be our ally, knowing that within every moment of uncertainty lies an opportunity for growth and self-discovery.

And so, dear reader, as you embark on your own path of transformation, remember that fear is not a roadblock but a stepping stone towards a more courageous existence. Embrace it, learn from it, and allow it to propel you forward, for beyond the shadows of fear lies the radiant light of courage, waiting patiently for you to embrace its warmth.

Thriving in Change

As I sat down to write this subchapter, I couldn't help but reflect on my own journey of embracing change. Change is inevitable, that much is certain. It sweeps us off our feet, leaving us uncertain and vulnerable. But what if, instead of resisting, we learned to navigate the tide of change with grace and resilience? What if we could transform ourselves and create a fulfilling life amidst the chaos? This subchapter is dedicated to just that - encouraging readers to thrive in times of change.

The problem, you see, lies not in change itself, but in our resistance to it. We become so attached to the comfort and familiarity of our routines that we close ourselves off to the endless possibilities that change brings. We fear the unknown, we fear failure, and most of all, we fear losing control. But what if I told you that by surrendering control, you could gain so much more?

Change, in its essence, is an opportunity for growth. It challenges us to step out of our comfort zones and discover strengths we never knew existed within us. It pushes us to adapt, to learn, and to evolve. In times of change, we are tested not only in our ability to survive but in our capacity to thrive. It is during these transformative moments that we have the power to redefine ourselves, to shape our own destiny.

Adapting is key. Just as a seedling must adjust and face the unknown as it emerges from the safety of the soil, we too must embrace change as an integral part of our personal development. It is during these times of change that we have the opportunity to shed old habits and beliefs that no longer serve us. We can cultivate new skills, forge new relationships, and discover passions that light our souls ablaze. Change should not be seen as a roadblock but as an invitation to explore new paths, to embark on adventures we may have never considered otherwise.

But how, you may ask, can we navigate the labyrinth of change with confidence and resilience? Firstly, we must surrender to the natural flow of life. Like a river carving its new course, we must let go of resistance and trust that change is guiding us towards something greater. Instead of clinging to the past, we must learn to live in the present, fully embracing each moment as it unfolds. By shifting our perspective from fear to curiosity, we cultivate a mindset that welcomes change as an opportunity for growth.

Secondly, we must cultivate self-awareness. Change can be overwhelming, and it is during these times that our sense of self can become fragmented. By taking the time to reflect on our values, passions, and purpose, we can anchor ourselves amidst the storm of change. Self-awareness empowers us to make intentional choices and navigate change in alignment with our deepest desires.

Finally, support systems are crucial. Surrounding ourselves with like-minded individuals who believe in our potential can be a powerful tool for thriving in change. They can provide guidance, accountability, and the encouragement we need to keep pushing forward. By seeking out mentors, joining communities of growth-minded individuals, and nurturing our most important relationships, we create a solid foundation from which we can flourish.

Embrace transformation, dear reader. Embrace it with all your heart and soul. Let it shape you, mold you, and guide you towards a life of purpose and fulfillment. Change is not something to be feared, but something to be celebrated. When we learn to thrive amidst the chaos, we unlock our infinite potential and become architects of our own destiny. So, take a deep breath, and let the winds of change carry you towards a future that surpasses your wildest dreams.

10

Finding Closure

The Importance of Closure

Closure.

A single word, but one that carries with it a weight so heavy that it can sometimes feel unbearable. The concept of closure has haunted me for years, lingering in the depths of my thoughts like a ghostly reminder of unfinished business. It was only recently, after years of soul-searching and countless sleepless nights, that I came to realize the true significance of closure in relationships.

When a relationship ends, whether it be a romantic partnership or a friendship, there is often a sense of unresolved emotions that linger in the aftermath. These emotions, if left unattended, can fester and grow, poisoning our hearts and minds. Finding closure is essential in order to break free from the shackles of the past and move forward with our lives.

Closure grants us the opportunity to make sense of what has transpired, to gain clarity and understanding. It allows us to process our emotions and come to terms with the end of the relationship. Without closure, we are left with a jumble of unanswered questions and unresolved feelings that continue to haunt us, preventing us from fully healing and moving on.

But closure is not just about tying up loose ends and finding answers. It goes much deeper than that. It is an opportunity for personal growth and transformation. Through seeking closure, we challenge ourselves to confront our inner demons and face our fears head-on. We learn to accept our vulnerabilities and weaknesses, and ultimately become stronger individuals.

Closure also paves the way for emotional well-being. It provides us with a sense of peace and closure, allowing us to release the emotional baggage that has burdened us for far too long. By finding closure, we are able to let go of resentments, anger, and pain, and create space for healing and forgiveness. It is only through this process that we can truly find inner peace and start anew.

Research has shown that closure can have a profound impact on our overall well-being. According to a study conducted by the University of California, individuals who actively sought closure in relationships reported higher levels of life satisfaction and lower levels of depression and anxiety. Closure, it seems, is not just a fancy word; it is a powerful tool that we all possess, capable of transforming our lives for the better.

So, how do we find closure? It is a journey unique to each individual, but there are some strategies that can assist us along the way. Journaling, for instance, can be an effective means of self-reflection and exploration. By writing down our thoughts and feelings, we gain a clearer understanding of our emotions and can begin to make sense of our experiences.

Therapy and counseling can also be invaluable resources in the search for closure. Working with a professional can provide us with guidance, support, and an objective perspective. Through therapy, we can navigate through the complexities of our emotions, develop coping strategies, and ultimately find the closure we so desperately seek.

In conclusion, closure is not just a fleeting desire; it is a vital component of our emotional well-being and personal growth. It allows us to untangle the knots of our past, find meaning in our experiences, and create space for healing and forgiveness. By seeking closure, we embark on a transformative journey that can lead us to a place of inner peace and fulfillment. And so, I invite you to embark on this journey with me, as we delve deeper into the significance of closure and explore the path to finding it.

Closure Rituals and Practices

When it's over, there is a void that remains. A gaping hole in your heart that yearns to be filled. You long for closure, a way to make sense of the chaos, to find peace within the storm. This is where closure rituals and practices come into play.

Every individual seeks closure in their own way, and what works for one may not work for another. This is why it is crucial to create personalized rituals that cater to your specific needs and emotions. Through these rituals, you can begin to find solace and move forward in your healing journey.

Take a moment to reflect on what closure means to you. Is it a sense of acceptance? Forgiveness? Letting go? Understanding your own needs and desires is the first step in creating a meaningful closure ritual.

One powerful closure ritual is writing a letter. Pour your heart out onto paper, expressing your thoughts, emotions, and frustrations. Let the words flow freely, releasing the burdens that weigh you down. You may choose to send this letter or keep it for yourself, but the act of putting your feelings into words can be incredibly cathartic.

Another helpful practice is creating a physical symbol of closure. This could be a collage of memories, a symbolic object, or even a ceremonial burning of mementos. By actively engaging in the physical realm, you are allowing yourself to let go and move forward.

Meditation and mindfulness exercises are also valuable tools for finding closure. Take the time to sit in stillness, breathing deeply and allowing your thoughts to flow freely. Explore the emotions that arise and gently release them, embracing a sense of calm and tranquility. This practice can help you gain clarity and perspective on the situation, aiding in the process of closure.

The final piece of advice I offer in this subchapter is to seek support. Closure is not a journey that should be embarked upon in isolation. Surround yourself with a community of compassionate individuals who can empathize with your experiences. Whether it is through therapy, support groups, or close friends and family, having a network of support can make all the difference.

As you embark on your own closure rituals and practices, remember that healing takes time. There is no set timeline for closure, and it is essential to be patient with yourself. Allow the process to unfold naturally, trusting that you are on the path towards healing and growth.

In the next chapter, we will delve deeper into the concept of forgiveness and how it plays a vital role in the closure process. But for now, take a moment to reflect on the closure rituals and practices that resonate with you. Begin to build a toolbox of techniques that will aid you in finding closure, knowing that you have the power to heal and move forward in your own time.

Forgiveness and Release

I have always believed that forgiveness is a vital part of healing. Throughout my life, I have witnessed how holding onto grudges and resentments can weigh us down, trapping us in a cycle of anger and bitterness. But I have also come to understand that forgiveness is not always easy; it requires a deep inner strength and a willingness to let go.

One strategy I have found helpful is to shift my perspective. Instead of dwelling on the hurt and pain caused by others, I try to see them as flawed human beings, just like myself. I remind myself that everyone makes mistakes and that holding onto anger only perpetuates my own suffering. By choosing to forgive, I am not condoning their actions; rather, I am freeing myself from the burden of carrying resentment.

Another technique that has helped me release resentment is practicing empathy. When we can put ourselves in someone else's shoes, we begin to understand the complexities of their actions. It becomes easier to empathize with their struggles and realize that their behavior may stem from their own pain and insecurities. This realization allows us to let go of anger and find compassion instead.

Journaling has also been a powerful tool in my journey towards forgiveness and release. By writing down my thoughts and emotions, I am able to explore and confront my own feelings of resentment. I delve deep into the reasons behind my anger, questioning whether it truly serves me. Through this process, I gain insights into my own wounds and discover the need for self-compassion. In turn, this allows me to extend that understanding and forgiveness to others.

One technique that may seem counterintuitive but has proven incredibly transformative is practicing gratitude. When we focus on what we are grateful for, we shift our attention away from the hurt and resentment that may be consuming us. By actively seeking out the good in our lives, we reframe our perspective and open ourselves up to forgiveness. Gratitude helps us find peace within ourselves and ultimately allows us to release the grip of anger and resentment.

Lastly, it is important to remember that forgiveness is a journey, not a destination. It is a process that takes time and self-reflection. Sometimes, we may forgive and release, only to find ourselves revisiting those emotions later. But that is okay. Each time we encounter these feelings, we have an opportunity to further heal and grow.

In conclusion, forgiveness and release are integral parts of finding closure. They provide us with the tools to let go of resentment and find peace within ourselves. By shifting our perspective, practicing empathy, journaling, practicing gratitude, and acknowledging forgiveness as a journey, we can free ourselves from the grip of anger and find the closure we seek. It is through forgiveness that we can truly move forward and start anew.

Honoring the Past, Embracing the Future

As I sat down at my cluttered desk, surrounded by piles of research papers and stacks of old photographs, I couldn't help but feel a sense of nostalgia wash over me. It was as if the room itself held a collection of memories, each one telling a story of a bygone era. I had always been drawn to history, fascinated by the stories of those who came before me and the lessons they left behind.

Honoring the past, I believed, was not just about preserving memories or celebrating tradition. It was about learning from the mistakes and triumphs of those who paved the way before us. It was about acknowledging the sacrifices made, the hardships endured, and the progress achieved. In doing so, we can gain valuable insights into the world we live in today and shape a better future.

In my research, I delved into the lives of historical figures who had impacted society in profound ways. Their stories were a tapestry of inspiration, resilience, and transformation. As I immersed myself in their narratives, I began to see parallels between their struggles and the challenges we faced today. Their triumphs gave me hope, their failures taught me humility, and their perseverance reminded me of the strength within each of us.

But honoring the past was not just about studying the lives of others; it was about acknowledging our own personal histories. For me, this meant reflecting on my own past and the experiences that had shaped me into the person I was today. It meant embracing the lessons I had learned, both the triumphs and the failures, and using them to guide my future path.

As I looked back on my journey, I realized that without honoring my past, I could never truly embrace my future. It was in the process of connecting with my roots that I discovered a sense of grounding and purpose. I could draw strength from the struggles of my ancestors, knowing that their perseverance ran through my veins. I could find solace in the stories of their triumphs, knowing that their legacy lived on in me.

In integrating the lessons learned from history into my own life, I found a sense of resolution. It was as if I had finally come to terms with the mistakes, regrets, and missed opportunities that had haunted me for so long. By embracing the past, I was able to release the weight that had been holding me back and move forward with a renewed sense of purpose.

Honoring the past and embracing the future merged together seamlessly. The stories of those who had come before us served as a guiding light, illuminating the obstacles we may face and offering wisdom for overcoming them. The lessons learned from our personal histories provided a compass, pointing us towards the path of fulfillment and growth.

In this subchapter, I invite readers to embark on a journey of self-discovery and reflection. As we explore the importance of honoring the past while embracing the future, we will delve into the intricate tapestry of history. We will unravel the threads of our own personal narratives, seeking resolution and a deeper understanding of who we truly are.

Let us learn from the mistakes and triumphs of those who have walked this earth before us. Let us bring their stories to life, weaving them into the fabric of our own existence. And let us step boldly into the future, armed with the knowledge, wisdom, and resolution to create a world that honors the past while embracing the future.

Creating a New Narrative

But deep down, beneath the layers of sorrow and despair, a voice whispered to me with a glimmer of hope. It was a voice that urged me to create a new narrative for myself, to redefine my identity and embrace a brighter future.

And so, I embarked on a journey of self-discovery, armed with determination and a fervent desire to rewrite the story of my life. I sought guidance from therapists, self-help books, and the internet – devouring any resource that promised to unveil the secrets of transforming my existence. In my research, I stumbled upon a subchapter that particularly resonated with me – one that encouraged readers like myself to craft a new narrative after finding closure. This chapter, filled with inspiration and vital guidance, ignited a spark within me that had long lain dormant.

The first step in creating a new narrative was to acknowledge the pain that held me captive in the past. I recognized that my experiences, though challenging, had shaped me into the person I had become. Through acceptance and forgiveness, I could release the grip of the past and move towards a future filled with promise.

With newfound clarity, I began to dream again. I allowed my imagination to soar, envisioning the life I desired for myself – a life free from the shackles of past mistakes and regrets. It was in these dreams that I discovered my true passions and aspirations, weaving them into the fabric of my renewed narrative.

As I unraveled the threads of my past, I embraced the opportunity to redefine my identity. I took stock of my strengths, acknowledging the resilience that had carried me through countless trials. I recognized the power within me to shape my own story, to choose which chapters I would write and which I would let go.

But creating a new narrative required more than just words on a page. It demanded action, a willingness to step outside of my comfort zone and embrace the unknown. I sought out new experiences, attempting things I had once considered impossible. With each small triumph, I gained confidence and began to see the vast potential that lay within me.

Throughout my journey, I encountered setbacks and moments of doubt. There were times when it seemed easier to retreat into the safety of my old narrative, to relive the familiar pain that had become like a worn-out security blanket. But I persevered, determined to write a new story that would empower me.

And as I continued to craft my new narrative, an extraordinary thing happened – I began to attract people who believed in me and supported my transformation. I found mentors who encouraged me to embrace my gifts and chase my dreams. Their steadfast belief in my abilities became a beacon of light, guiding me through the darkest moments.

Creating a new narrative was not a one-time event, but a lifelong journey of constant growth and reinvention. It required compassion for myself, recognizing that I was allowed to stumble and make mistakes along the way. It demanded resilience and unwavering dedication to my vision.

With each passing day, the old narrative continued to fade, becoming nothing more than a distant memory. In its place, I discovered a story of resilience, strength, and limitless possibility. Through creating a new narrative, I had transformed my life, rewriting the script to one of hope, self-discovery, and an unwavering belief in the power of embracing a brighter future.

11

∿

Building a Better Future

Setting Intentions and Goals

It was in this moment of introspection that I stumbled upon a subchapter in a book titled "Setting Intentions and Goals." Intrigued by the idea of finding clarity and purpose, I delved into the pages, hoping to unearth the guidance I so desperately needed.

The words within the subchapter emphasized the importance of setting intentions and goals for the future. It was explained that without a clear vision of where we wanted to go, we would stumble through life, never fully realizing our potential. It was like trying to navigate a dense forest without a map; we would wander aimlessly, getting lost in the vast expanse of possibilities.

But how could I begin to clarify my vision and set actionable steps towards personal growth? The book offered a step-by-step process that would help me unravel the chaos of my scattered thoughts and pave the way towards a more purposeful existence.

First and foremost, it stressed the significance of self-reflection. Only by looking inward could I truly understand my desires, strengths, and weaknesses. It was through deep introspection that I would find the clarity needed to set meaningful intentions and goals. This required taking the time, away from the noise and distractions of the outside world, to listen to the whispers of my own heart.

The book urged me to ask myself thought-provoking questions, such as "What brings me joy?" and "What am I passionate about?" These inquiries served as compass points, guiding me towards a vision that resonated with my truest self.

Once I had gained some insight into my desires and passions, the book encouraged me to brainstorm specific goals that would support my vision. These goals needed to be SMART - Specific, Measurable, Achievable, Relevant, and Time-bound. By setting tangible milestones, I would be better equipped to track my progress and stay on course.

However, simply setting goals was not enough; I needed to take action. The book emphasized the importance of breaking down my goals into smaller, more manageable tasks. By doing so, I would be less overwhelmed and more likely to make consistent progress towards my aspirations.

It also advised me to embrace the power of visualization and affirmation. By vividly imagining myself achieving my goals, I could tap into the boundless potential of my mind. Additionally, repeating positive affirmations would help reprogram my subconscious beliefs, reinforcing the belief that I was capable of achieving my dreams.

As I closed the book, I knew there was no turning back. The subchapter had illuminated a path before me, one that promised clarity, purpose, and personal growth. It was time for me to set intentions and goals that would guide my journey towards a more fulfilled life. It was time for me to take the actionable steps necessary to transform my dreams into reality.

Embracing Independence and Self-Sufficiency

To fully grasp the concept of self-sufficiency, I delved into extensive research. I discovered that embracing independence means taking ownership of my thoughts, actions, and decisions. It requires me to cultivate a deep sense of self-awareness and trust in my own capabilities. It invites me to acknowledge that I have the power to shape my own destiny and create a life that aligns with my true desires.

However, this journey towards independence is not without its challenges. It requires me to confront my fears, insecurities, and doubts head-on. It asks me to step out of my comfort zone and explore uncharted territories. But in doing so, I discovered that true growth and fulfillment lie just beyond the boundaries of familiarity.

One of the key aspects of embracing independence is learning how to be self-reliant. It means developing the skills, knowledge, and resources necessary to navigate life's ups and downs. I began by identifying my strengths and weaknesses, then actively sought opportunities to enhance my abilities and develop new ones.

I also realized that self-sufficiency does not mean isolating oneself from others. On the contrary, it entails surrounding oneself with a supportive network of individuals who share similar values and goals. These individuals become the pillars of strength and encouragement necessary to stay on the path of independence.

Creating a fulfilling life on my own terms demanded a shift in mindset. It meant letting go of societal expectations and embracing my true passions and aspirations. I stopped seeking validation from others and instead focused on nurturing my inner desires. I cultivated a deep sense of purpose and began carving my own path towards success.

In this subchapter, readers will find practical strategies and exercises to help them embrace independence and self-sufficiency. They will learn the importance of setting boundaries and practicing self-care. They will explore how to overcome self-doubt and cultivate resilience. They will also discover the power of goal-setting and the art of adapting to change.

Ultimately, embracing independence and self-sufficiency is a lifelong journey. It requires constant self-reflection, growth, and adaptation. It is not a destination but rather a way of life. As readers delve into the world of self-reliance, they will unlock the immense power within themselves and discover a life that is truly fulfilling and authentic.

Cultivating Resilience and Adaptability

Problem: Life is full of unexpected twists and turns, and we often find ourselves grappling with adversity and setbacks. Whether it's the loss of a job, a breakup, or a major disappointment, these challenges can quickly knock us off course and leave us feeling helpless and defeated.

Solution: Cultivating resilience and adaptability is key to overcoming these obstacles and thriving in the face of adversity. It allows us to bounce back from setbacks, learn from our mistakes, and embrace change with open arms.

In my own journey, I've encountered countless hurdles and moments of despair. Each time I faced a setback, I realized the importance of resilience and adaptability in reclaiming control over my life. The strategies I've discovered along the way have helped me not only navigate the hardships but also emerge stronger and more resilient than ever before.

One effective strategy is reframing setbacks as opportunities for growth. Instead of viewing a setback as a failure, it's crucial to see it as a chance to learn and improve. This mindset shift allows us to approach challenges with curiosity and a willingness to evolve. By reframing setbacks in this way, we can extract valuable lessons and turn adversity into stepping stones towards success.

Another powerful strategy is practicing self-care and building a support network. Taking care of our physical, emotional, and mental well-being is crucial for building resilience. Prioritizing self-care activities such as exercise, meditation, and hobbies can help us recharge and stay resilient in the face of challenges. Additionally, having a network of supportive individuals who can provide guidance, encouragement, and a listening ear can greatly enhance our ability to bounce back and adapt to change.

Moreover, embracing uncertainty and being open to change is essential in cultivating resilience and adaptability. Life is constantly evolving, and resisting change only hinders our growth. By embracing uncertainties and being flexible in our approach, we open ourselves up to new opportunities and possibilities. This willingness to adapt not only allows us to thrive in the face of adversity but also fosters personal growth and development.

Lastly, it's vital to cultivate a growth mindset. Believing in our ability to learn and grow from challenges rather than being defined by them is key to building resilience and adaptability. By adopting a growth mindset, we become more resilient in the face of setbacks and are able to approach obstacles with tenacity and perseverance.

As I continue on my journey of cultivating resilience and adaptability, I've come to realize that setbacks and challenges are inevitable parts of life. However, how we respond to them and the strategies we use to navigate through them can make all the difference. By reframing setbacks as learning experiences, practicing self-care, embracing change, and adopting a growth mindset, we can not only overcome challenges but also thrive in the face of adversity.

Embracing Personal Passions and Hobbies

I had found myself trapped in this cycle for years, desperately longing for something more. It wasn't until I stumbled upon an article discussing the importance of embracing personal passions and hobbies that I realized the key to breaking free from this suffocating monotony. Intrigued, I delved deeper into the subject, pouring over books, research papers, and interviews in search of answers.

This subchapter, aptly titled "Embracing Personal Passions and Hobbies," aims to guide readers through the process of discovering and pursuing activities that bring them genuine joy and fulfillment. It offers not just a mere glimpse, but an in-depth exploration into the power of nurturing our personal interests.

But first, we must address the problem at hand. The problem is twofold: the lack of awareness of our passions and the fear of pursuing them. Many of us have forgotten what truly brings us joy, blinded by the demands and distractions of everyday life. We have become disconnected from our true selves, existing rather than truly living. We have convinced ourselves that our passions and hobbies are luxuries, that they have no place in the hustle and bustle of the real world. We fear the unknown and the potential failure that comes with pursuing our deepest desires.

The solution lies in the power of self-discovery and the courage to pursue our passions. The first step is to take a moment to reflect on what truly brings us joy, what sets our soul on fire. This can be anything from painting to playing a musical instrument, from cooking to writing. It doesn't matter what the activity is, as long as it brings us a deep sense of fulfillment.

Once we have identified our passions, the next step is to make time for them. Often, we use the excuse of not having enough time as a means to avoid pursuing our interests. But let me tell you this, dear reader, time is what we make of it. We must carve out moments in our busy days, even if it means waking up an hour earlier or sacrificing a few episodes of our favorite TV show. Dedicate that time solely to our passions, immersing ourselves fully in the joy and creativity they bring.

Another obstacle we must address is the fear of failure. We worry that we won't be good enough, that our efforts will be in vain. But I urge you to remember this: our passions and hobbies are not about achieving perfection, but about the journey itself. It is the process of exploration and growth that brings us true fulfillment. So, let go of the fear of failure, embrace the possibility of making mistakes, and allow yourself to learn and grow through your chosen activities.

In this subchapter, readers will find not just inspiration, but practical guidance on how to embrace their passions and hobbies. From journaling exercises to help uncover hidden interests, to tips on overcoming self-doubt, to stories of individuals who have found true happiness through pursuing their passions, every page is filled with encouragement and empowerment.

Through my own journey of self-discovery and the countless stories of those I have encountered, I have learned one vital truth: embracing our personal passions and hobbies is not a luxury, but a necessity. It is through this pursuit that we tap into our authenticity, find solace in our chaotic world, and experience true joy. So, dear reader, allow yourself the freedom to explore your passions, and watch as your life transforms into something truly remarkable.

Creating a Life of Meaning and Purpose

After the end of a relationship, it is not uncommon to feel lost and adrift, unsure of how to move forward without the person who once played a significant role in your life. It is during these times of transition and reflection that the opportunity arises to redefine who you are and what you want out of life. This subchapter aims to inspire and guide readers on their journey towards creating a life of meaning and purpose, one that aligns their actions with their personal values and aspirations.

As I found myself in the aftermath of my own breakup, I was faced with the daunting task of rediscovering who I was outside of that relationship. It was a blank canvas, awaiting the strokes of my own intentions and desires. I delved deep into a period of introspection, exploring my core values and reflecting on what truly brought me joy and fulfillment.

One of the key insights I discovered during this process was the importance of aligning my actions with my personal values. I realized that I had spent too much time living according to the expectations of others, rather than living in accordance with my own authentic self. This subchapter encourages readers to do the same - to take a step back and evaluate their actions, ensuring that they are in line with their own values and aspirations.

To create a life of meaning and purpose, it is essential to reconnect with your passions and interests. What brings you joy? What sparks your curiosity? Identifying these aspects of your life will guide you towards a fulfilling path. For me, it was writing. I found solace in expressing my thoughts and emotions through words, and as I began to dedicate more time to my craft, I felt a sense of purpose that I hadn't experienced before.

However, creating a life of meaning and purpose is not solely about individual pursuits. It is equally important to cultivate connections with others who share your values and aspirations. Surrounding yourself with like-minded individuals who support and inspire you will further fuel your journey towards a more fulfilling existence. I found solace in joining writing communities and attending workshops, where I was able to connect with fellow creatives and immerse myself in a supportive network.

As you embark on this transformative journey, it is crucial to remember that it is okay to take your time and be patient with yourself. Creating a life of meaning and purpose is not an overnight process; it is a continuous exploration and refinement of who you are and what you truly want out of life. Embrace the joys and challenges along the way, and trust in your own ability to create a life that is aligned with your values and aspirations.

In conclusion, after the end of a relationship, there lies a great opportunity for growth and self-discovery. This subchapter aims to inspire and guide readers towards creating a life of meaning and purpose by aligning their actions with their personal values and aspirations. Through introspection, reconnecting with passions, and cultivating connections with like-minded individuals, the path towards a fulfilling existence becomes clearer. Remember to be patient and trust in your own journey, for the canvas of life is yours to paint.

12

The Journey Continues

Embracing Self-Reflection

As I sat down to write this subchapter, I couldn't help but feel a sense of anticipation. Self-reflection has always been a cornerstone of my personal journey, a tool that has allowed me to understand myself better and make better choices in life. And now, I have the opportunity to share this wisdom with others.

One of the most profound realizations I have had through self-reflection is the understanding that our desires, values, and aspirations are not fixed entities. They are ever-evolving, shaped by our experiences, interactions, and the shifting tides of life. It is through self-reflection that we can tap into the depths of our being and uncover our true desires, align with our core values, and nurture our aspirations.

To embark on this journey of self-reflection, one must be willing to dig deep. It is not a task for the faint of heart, for it requires the courage to face our fears, insecurities, and vulnerabilities. But within this journey lies the promise of transformation, of a life lived in greater alignment with our authentic selves.

The first step in embracing self-reflection is creating a safe space for introspection. This space can be physical, such as a cozy corner in your home or a favorite café, or it can be a sacred space within your mind. It is a space where you can be vulnerable, a space where you can let your thoughts flow freely without fear of judgment. In this space, you can begin to explore the depths of your desires, values, and aspirations.

Once you have created this safe space, the next step is to start asking yourself the tough questions. What do you truly desire in life? What are the values that guide your decisions and actions? What are your aspirations, the dreams that you hold dear to your heart? By delving deep into these questions, you can start to unravel the layers of conditioning and societal expectations that may have masked your true desires.

As you engage in self-reflection, it is important to approach this process with curiosity and an open mind. Don't be afraid to challenge your assumptions and beliefs. Allow yourself to explore different perspectives and possibilities. In doing so, you might discover desires and aspirations you never knew existed, or you might find that some of your current aspirations no longer resonate with your true self. Self-reflection is not a one-time activity; it is an ongoing journey of discovery and growth.

In embracing self-reflection, we give ourselves permission to be our own best friend, therapist, and guide. We become the architects of our own lives, actively shaping our dreams and aspirations. Through self-reflection, we can align our actions with our values, making choices that are true to our authentic selves.

So, dear reader, as we embark on this journey together, I invite you to embrace self-reflection wholeheartedly. Dive deep into the depths of your being, explore the vast landscape of your desires, values, and aspirations.

Shed the layers that no longer serve you and embrace the authenticity that lies within. It is through self-reflection that we can truly blossom into the best version of ourselves.

Celebrating Progress and Milestones

When we celebrate our progress, we are reinforcing positive behavior and reinforcing the belief in ourselves. It serves as a reminder that we are capable of overcoming obstacles and achieving our goals. I remember the first time I accomplished a significant milestone in my personal growth journey. It was a moment of immense pride and joy, where I felt a surge of confidence and motivation. From that experience, I realized that celebrating my progress plays a crucial role in my continued growth and success.

Acknowledging achievements is not about being complacent or settling; rather, it is about recognizing the efforts we have put in and the growth we have experienced. Celebrating our milestones allows us to reflect on the challenges we have overcome and the skills we have developed along the way. It gives us a chance to appreciate the hard work and dedication it took to reach where we are now.

Beyond personal fulfillment, celebrating progress and milestones can also have a positive impact on our overall well-being. Studies have shown that celebrating achievements releases dopamine, the neurotransmitter responsible for feelings of pleasure and reward. By celebrating, we are boosting our mood and increasing our motivation to continue striving towards bigger and better goals. The celebration becomes a fuel for future growth and a reminder of our potential.

Embracing a sense of accomplishment is not a form of self-indulgence but rather a way of cultivating a growth mindset. When we embrace our accomplishments, we are creating a positive environment for ourselves. We are affirming that we are capable of achieving greatness. This positive mindset not only promotes personal growth but also attracts more opportunities and success into our lives.

So how can we celebrate our progress and milestones effectively? It is important to find ways that resonate with us personally. Whether it is treating ourselves to a day of self-care, sharing our achievements with loved ones, or even documenting our progress in a journal, the key is to find activities that bring us joy, reflection, and a sense of pride. It is essential to celebrate both big and small milestones, as each step forward is a worthy achievement.

In conclusion, celebrating progress and milestones in our personal growth journey is crucial for our ongoing development. It reinforces positive behavior, acknowledges our achievements, and boosts our motivation and confidence. By embracing a sense of accomplishment, we cultivate a growth mindset and create a positive environment for ourselves. So, let us take a moment to reflect on how far we have come, celebrate our achievements, and continue moving forward with renewed determination and enthusiasm.

Cultivating Gratitude and Joy

As I sat down to write this subchapter, I couldn't help but feel a sense of excitement and intrigue. The topic of cultivating gratitude and joy spoke directly to my soul, for I had spent a significant portion of my life striving to find beauty and positivity amidst the challenges that came my way. It was a journey that had led me to discover profound insights and transformative strategies, which I was eager to share with others.

When life throws us curveballs, it's easy to get caught up in the negative aspects of our situation. We dwell on what has gone wrong, how unfair it all seems, and the endless what-ifs that haunt our thoughts. But what if we approached challenges from a different perspective? What if, instead of focusing on what we lack, we shifted our attention to what we have?

Gratitude is a powerful force, capable of transforming our entire outlook on life. It teaches us to appreciate the smallest of blessings, to find solace and contentment in the present moment. It broadens our horizons, allowing us to see beyond the difficulties that surround us. Through my own experiences, I've learned that cultivating gratitude is not merely a state of mind but a deliberate practice, one that requires conscious effort and commitment.

One strategy I discovered along my journey was the practice of keeping a gratitude journal. Each night before bed, I would list at least three things I was grateful for that day. Some nights, it was as simple as the warmth of a cup of tea, the sound of rain on my window, or the smile of a loved one. Other nights, it was the resilience I found within myself to overcome an obstacle or the opportunity to learn something new. In time, this daily practice became a ritual, an anchor that reminded me of the beauty that existed even in the darkest of times.

But gratitude alone is not enough; we must also cultivate joy. Joy is like a radiant beam of light that pierces through the clouds of despair. It's a state of being that allows us to find happiness and contentment, regardless of our circumstances. However, joy is not something that can be forced or manufactured. It is a byproduct of gratitude, authenticity, and inner alignment.

In my research, I came across a study that demonstrated the power of finding joy in the midst of challenges. Participants were asked to practice daily acts of kindness for others, even when they themselves were facing difficult circumstances. The results were remarkable. Those who practiced kindness reported higher levels of joy and satisfaction with their lives, despite their own struggles. This finding speaks volumes about the transformative nature of spreading positivity and seeking opportunities to bring joy to others.

The pursuit of gratitude and joy is not a one-size-fits-all endeavor. It requires us to explore different avenues of personal growth and self-discovery. For some, it may mean delving into the world of art, music, or nature. For others, it may involve practicing mindfulness, engaging in acts of kindness, or spending time with loved ones. The key is to be open to new experiences, to venture outside our comfort zones, and to embrace the joy that lies hidden amidst the chaos.

As you embark on this journey of cultivating gratitude and joy, remember that it is not about denying or suppressing the challenges you face. It is about finding strength, beauty, and solace in the midst of adversity. It is about realizing that even in the darkest of times, there is always something to be grateful for, something to bring a smile to your face. So, dear reader, take a deep breath, open your heart, and let the beauty of gratitude and joy guide you towards a fulfilling life.

Embracing New Beginnings

To truly embrace new beginnings, one must first acknowledge that endings are an inevitable part of life. They come in various forms - the end of a relationship, the conclusion of a chapter in our careers, or the closing of a door on a dream that is no longer sustainable. These endings can leave us feeling lost, uncertain, and vulnerable. However, it is in those moments of transition that we have the opportunity to redefine ourselves, to shed old skin and grow into the person we are destined to become.

The solution lies in cultivating a mindset of openness and a willingness to adapt. It is akin to standing at the edge of a precipice, toes curled over the ledge as we take a leap of faith into the unknown. It requires us to release the safety net of the familiar and embrace uncertainty with open arms. It is in this state of vulnerability that we discover our innate resilience, our capacity to not only survive but thrive in the face of adversity.

Through my own journey of embracing new beginnings, I have learned that change is not linear. It is a process that ebbs and flows, with moments of stagnation interspersed between bursts of growth. It is important to remember that change does not always come in grand gestures or dramatic transformations. Often, it is the small, incremental steps that lead us to profound shifts in our lives.

Research shows that those who actively seek out new beginnings and approach them with an open mind are more likely to experience personal growth, happiness, and success. Psychologists refer to this as the "growth mindset" - a belief that abilities and intelligence can be developed with effort and perseverance. This mindset allows us to view challenges as opportunities for growth rather than insurmountable obstacles.

Throughout the pages of this book, I will share my personal journey of embracing new beginnings - the triumphs, the setbacks, and everything in between. Together, we will explore practical strategies for navigating the unknown, cultivating resilience, and maintaining a sense of optimism in the face of uncertainty. My hope is that you, dear reader, will find inspiration, guidance, and a renewed sense of purpose as you embrace your own new beginnings.

The Power of Self-Love

Through my own experiences and extensive research, I had come to understand that self-love was not just a buzzword or a cliché phrase thrown around in self-help books. It was a profound and transformative force that had the potential to shape our lives in ways we could never imagine.

This final subchapter was intended to dig deep into the core of self-love, to unravel its mysteries and uncover its true power. It was a reminder of the inherent worth and beauty that resided within each and every one of us, waiting to be recognized and embraced.

In a world that often tells us we are not enough, self-love becomes an act of rebellion, a revolutionary act of self-acceptance and self-compassion. It allows us to break free from the chains of self-doubt and self-criticism, and instead, nurture a relationship of kindness and understanding with ourselves.

Research has consistently shown that individuals who practice self-love not only experience higher levels of happiness and fulfillment, but they also have better physical and mental health. When we truly love ourselves, we are more likely to engage in behaviors that promote our well-being, such as regular exercise, healthy eating, and getting enough rest.

But self-love is not just about taking care of our physical bodies. It goes much deeper than that. It is about cultivating a profound sense of self-compassion and acceptance, embracing our flaws and imperfections with grace.

In this final subchapter, I wanted to offer inspiration and guidance on how to cultivate self-love. It was not a one-size-fits-all approach, but rather a journey unique to each individual. It required patience, perseverance, and a willingness to look inward with honesty and vulnerability.

I shared stories of individuals who had journeyed through the darkest depths of self-loathing and emerged on the other side, bathed in the radiant light of self-love. Their stories were not just tales of triumph, but also reminders that self-love was not reserved for a select few; it was available to all who dared to believe in its power.

I delved into practical exercises and strategies that allowed readers to start their own journeys of self-love. I encouraged them to engage in daily affirmations, to practice self-care rituals that nourished their souls, and to surround themselves with people who celebrated their worth.

But above all, I reminded my readers that self-love was not just an external practice but an internal shift in mindset. It started with recognizing our worth and embracing our unique qualities. It was about forgiving ourselves for past mistakes and allowing ourselves the space to grow and evolve, knowing that we were deserving of love and acceptance every step of the way.

As I finished writing the closing lines of the subchapter on self-love, my heart swelled with a deep sense of fulfillment. It was my hope that this final piece of the book would be a guiding light for all those who read it, illuminating their path to a more meaningful and joyful life.

For in the end, it is through the power of self-love that we find the strength to persevere, to trust in our own abilities, and to courageously walk towards the life we have always imagined. And as the pages turned and the words resonated, I knew that this journey of self-love was just the beginning, for me and for all those who believed in its transformative power.